THE ART OF THE COOKIE

THE ART OF THE COOKIE

Over 75 Irresistible Recipes

By

JANN JOHNSON

Photography

HOLLY STEWART

CHRONICLE BOOKS

SAN FRANCISCO

Design by Palomine

Editing by Leslie Jonath and William LeBlond

Food Styling by Susan Devaty

Prop Styling by Thea Chalmers

Library of Congress Cataloging-in-Publication Data
Johnson, Jann.
    The Art of the Cookie: over 75 irresistible recipes / by
  Jann Johnson; photographs by Holly Stewart.
        p.   cm.
    Includes bibliographical references and index.
    ISBN 0-8118-0437-2
    1. Cookies.   I. Title.
  TX772.J62   1994
  641.8'654--dc20   94-866
                              CIP

Printed in Hong Kong.

ISBN 0-8118-0437-2

Distributed in Canada by Raincoast Books,
112 East Third Ave., Vancouver, B.C. V5T 1C8

10 9 8 7 6 5 4 3 2 1

Chronicle Books
275 Fifth Street
San Francisco, CA 94103

To the memory of my mother, Vivian Maureen McBeth Johnson

ACKNOWLEDGMENTS

With genuine appreciation for their help with this book,
I warmly thank all my friends and colleagues:

Jay Peterson, who helped create a beautiful presentation, and Elton Cantrell, for special assistance.

Jim Rhodes, David Dunlap, and Cathy Higgins, who helped get the ball rolling.

Judith Weber, my superb agent.

The talented Leslie Jonath and William LeBlond at Chronicle Books. Carolyn Miller, Laura Reily, and Carolyn Krebs, my insightful editors.

Holly Stewart, for her lovely photography.

Palomine, for their book design.

Susan Devaty, the food stylist.

Thea Chalmers, the prop stylist

Carol Barbera, for graciously typing pages of longhand.

Margaret Lancester, for transcribing the manuscript so well and for introducing me to computers. Robert Grehan, my PC trainer—just in time to fine tune the work.

Kathy Duffy and Aretha Cantrell for kindly testing recipes. Peter Hempel, Mary Randolph Carter, Liza Carter, Lynda Sanchez, Rafael Sanchez, and Catherine Bacon, for wonderful aesthetic feedback.

Mike Peck, for fine custom-made wooden tools.

In addition, my sincere thanks to the following:

Jim McGilloway, The Gilway Company, Ltd.

Lynda Glenn and Boyd Foster, Arrowhead Mills

Heidi Hovland, Hershey's (Fleishman-Hillard, Inc.)

Duncan Hayter and R. Wood, Tate & Lyle International

Mary Duffer, Reynolds Metals Company

Marlene Hronowski, Cook Flavoring Company

McCormick & Company

Nielsen Massey Vanillas

Ines Sepp, Sepp Leaf Products

Sally Selby, The Pillsbury Company

Heckers & Ceresota

The Quaker Oats Company

Josephine Angiuli, Domino Sugar

The Sugar Association

Golden Blossom Honey

Carol McClenahan, Milk Industry Foundation

Shelley Colvin, Land O'Lakes

American Dairy Association of Minnesota

Pittman & Davis

Blue Diamond Growers

Mauna Loa Macadamia Nut Corporation

The New York Public Library

The great team of volunteers who tasted and critiqued the cookies—friends, colleagues, taxi drivers, doormen, and neighbors.

CONTENTS

INTRODUCTION

I believe in small pleasures and old-fashioned, delicious homemade cookies are a personal favorite. They're a simple treat in a computer age of faxes and fast food. My elevator encounters in New York City are telling. One elevator, packed with tough young upstarts, became church quiet when I entered, carrying a handmade gingerbread castle. The gang of six turned into an entranced, curious audience of adorable kids. Another elevator, filled with serious power brokers in expensive suits, shifted attitude when I stepped in with a basket of fragrant, just-baked cookies for a photography shoot. Prompted by the aroma, nostalgic memories and wistful longings for homemade cookies were quickly murmured to me, a stranger.

There are generations of gifted cooks and bakers in my family. They were pioneers who settled in the west and carried their heirloom recipes with them. Hospitality went hand in hand with an offering of something delicious—and to me, it still does. When I was growing up, my family would visit our relatives in Texas between Air Force assignments abroad. During our stays, the mouth-watering country menu included hickory-smoked barbecue, hot savory corn bread, collard greens, chili pinto beans, cornmeal-battered fried catfish, and Grandfather E.A.'s spicy sage-garlic sausage, but the highlight was the unforgettable pies, cakes, tender sugar cookies, gingersnaps, and fat butterscotch pecan slices Grandmother Nellie made. They were set out on a cloth-covered table, ready for dessert, teatime, or any time. Many of the ingredients—thick cream, freshly churned butter, clabber, sour cream, and newly laid eggs—were from their farm, and the papershell pecans and fruit grew in the front yard. There, I learned some basic truths about baking—fresh, premium ingredients, a good recipe, and care in preparation produce excellent results.

My introduction to baking started around the age of seven. My mother knew that my curiosity about the chemical reaction of everyday ingredients turning into miraculous baked delights would be well served by this hands-on science lesson. We had just moved from living on a sugar cane farm in the tropics, so I knew firsthand about the origin of sugar, but I wondered about the other ingredients, as well (the biggest mystery was eggs). If each ingredient were cooked separately, minced, mixed with milk and baked would something similar result? Instinctively, I knew it wouldn't. My first try at baking resulted in a cake that looked like the Leaning Tower of Pisa frosted in Sci-Fi Technicolor (I had used every food color in the set, and then some). The dog took one look at it and said "No way"; ditto for Dad. The next baking attempt was drop sugar cookies. My father liked those, and my affection for baking cookies had begun. Through wonderful cookbooks (thank you, Julia), my talented Aunt Polly, and classes in London, Paris, and the United States, I continued to learn more about baking over the years.

Whether your own baking career is advanced or is just beginning, this collection of easy-to-make recipes and tips for success was created for you to enjoy, again and again. The recipes include classic chocolate chip and peanut butter cookies and some new ideas—such as boiled cider bars and mocha macadamia shortbread—to expand your repertoire.

Cookies are what I bake most often; they're a small treat compared to pie or cake, but satisfy a taste for something sweet. I like the ceremony of serving café au lait, tea, or cider steaming hot in a beautiful bone china cup, or something ice cold in an unusual glass, with cookies presented on a pretty plate served with a linen napkin—and sometimes, I even get the chance to do it. As professional chefs know, an appealing presentation of food adds to the pleasure and success of a dish.

Cookies may be mailed for a heart-warming gift from home or popped into a pocket for an alfresco treat. Fresh flowers and handmade cookies make a good, informal house guest present. Some cookies seem especially suited for certain times: soft molasses cookies for autumn tailgate picnics, crisp citrus wafers for beach days, and festive decorated cookies for birthday parties and holidays. Tiny cookies are an appreciated dessert at parties because they are graceful to eat (try several baskets of different flavors on a buffet table). Elegant cookies such as Florentines and chocolate madeleines, especially in miniature and served with espresso, are a proper end for a formal haute cuisine dinner. Even weddings are occasions for serving cookies; orange-almond cookies and heart-shaped cookies (perhaps monogrammed in icing) would be charming, and a handsome cupid cookie could top the wedding cake. Many cookies freeze well (noted in the recipes) to help full schedules. Ideas for wrapping cookies to give as gifts are given at the end of the book.

The Art of the Cookie will help make your cookie baking simple, creative, and enjoyable, and let you stack up many small pleasures of your own.

INGREDIENTS

For delectable cookies, use the best, freshest products available: grade AA creamery butter, pure vanilla extract (not imitation), new eggs, aromatic spices, and premium chocolate. Fine ingredients can be found in supermarkets, natural foods stores, specialty foods stores, and by mail. Check product dates and store ingredients appropriately to preserve their goodness. The following is a brief guide to the main ingredients used in this book.

FLOURS AND GRAINS

All-purpose flour, bleached or unbleached, is the mainstay of most cookie recipes. All-purpose flour is suitable for all types of baking because it is a blend of hard and soft wheats, each with its own baking properties. Hard wheat is higher in protein, which helps develop structure in baked goods; soft wheat is lower in protein and adds tenderness to cookies, pastries, and cakes. Some bakers prefer bleached flour because it is whiter and they claim it gives the best baking results. Others prefer unbleached flour because they like the straight-from-nature ivory color, the slightly higher amount of protein and vitamins, and are pleased with the baking results. I use both, but favor the unbleached.

Flour may absorb moisture in humid conditions. High humidity may call for a slight addition of flour to a recipe, while low humidity may require a slight reduction of flour. The only way to know is to test the recipe.

Store all-purpose flour in an airtight container in a cool, dry place. It also may be frozen, but allow it to come to room temperature before using.

Whole-wheat flour is more prone to spoilage than all-purpose flour, because it contains the wheat germ, which is high in oil that can turn rancid. If you don't use your whole-wheat flour often, it should be refrigerated or frozen in an airtight container. Allow it to come to room temperature before using.

Graham flour is a coarse-ground whole-wheat flour named after Sylvester Graham, the inventor of the grinding and milling process for whole-wheat flour. Regular whole-wheat flour may be used in place of graham flour.

Brown rice flour, available in natural foods stores and some supermarkets, adds a crunchy texture to cookies. According to Arrowhead Mills, "it seems to be the preferred grain of many insects," so refrigerate or freeze it in an airtight container, up to 6 months. Allow it to come to room temperature before using.

Old-fashioned whole-grain **rolled oats** are the best for baking. Quick, not instant, oats may also be substituted for old-fashioned rolled oats. Oats are nutritious and give an earthy flavor and texture to cookies. Store them in an airtight container.

Arrowroot comes from a tropical tuber that is dried and ground to a white powder. Similar in texture and appearance to cornstarch, arrowroot adds easily digestible nutrition and a crisp texture to cookies. Its name is derived from the legend that American Indians used it as a healing agent for arrow wounds.

Yellow, white, and even blue **cornmeal** is available in natural foods stores and supermarkets. Its color reflects the color of the corn ground for the meal. I prefer stone-ground cornmeal, but all types are suitable. Cornmeal has a relatively short shelf life, about 8 months if refrigerated. Store it airtight in the refrigerator or freezer if it will not be used within a month; let it come to room temperature before using.

LEAVENING

Baking powder and baking soda cause a chemical reaction that helps cookies rise. Double-acting baking powder means that there are two rising actions: The first happens when the baking powder combines with moisture (a good reason to always measure with a dry spoon), and the second rising action is activated by the heat of the oven. Baking powder has an approximate shelf life of one year. To check baking powder for freshness, mix a pinch of it with a spoonful of hot water; if it bubbles fiercely, it's still good.

Baking soda, a multipurpose product, is a single-acting leavener that starts reacting as soon as liquid comes in contact with it, so batter containing baking soda should be baked directly after mixing. Baking soda has a very long shelf life in dry conditions.

In this book, **cream of tartar** is used in recipes containing a large percentage of egg whites, such as royal icing and meringues, to help add stability.

Store baking powder, baking soda, and cream of tartar airtight in a cool, dark place.

SUGARS AND SWEETENERS

Granulated sugar is refined from sugar cane or sugar beets. There is a difference of quality in brands; I often buy the best in economical 25-pound bags.

Superfine sugar is a finely granulated sugar sometimes used in meringues. Because superfine sugar can be expensive, I sometimes make my own by pulsing granulated sugar in the food processor or blender.

Confectioners' sugar (also known as powdered sugar or icing sugar) is the finest granulation of sugar widely available to the public; it has a small amount (3 percent) of cornstarch to help keep the fine sugar grains from clumping together. Always sift confectioners' sugar after measuring (unless mentioned otherwise) to remove any lumps.

Light brown sugar, also known as golden sugar, is granulated sugar with molasses added. **Dark brown sugar** has approximately double the amount of molasses that light brown sugar has. Both kinds have a tendency to harden, especially dark brown sugar. (I rarely buy it in quantity.)

Ecru-colored **maple sugar** is the result of removing the water from maple syrup. It is a joy to use in cookies when the flavor of maple is wanted but the stickiness of maple syrup is not. Maple sugar is granulated in texture and doesn't have to be firmly packed like brown sugars. Some natural foods stores carry it, and it is listed in the mail-order guide on page 116.

All sugars may be stored indefinitely in airtight containers, in a dark cool place.

Unsulfured molasses is a syrup made from boiled sugar cane and/or sugar beet sugar (dissolved in water) in its initial refining process. Sulfured molasses is made at a later point (as a by-product) and has an off taste.

Black treacle is a thick, dark, faintly sulfured molasses-type cane syrup with a smoky, exotic flavor. Used primarily by the British for their famous treacle tarts, gingerbread, and parkin, it is available at specialty foods stores.

Maple syrup is the sweet sap from the sugar maple tree, boiled to concentrate the flavor.

Cane sugar syrup, also known as golden syrup, is a delicious sweet syrup made from sugar cane juice and is available in some supermarkets. It is similar to (and often interchanged with) light **corn syrup**, a sweet syrup derived from corn.

Honey, the bee's sensuous contribution to the world of sweetenings, has a range of flavors depending on the source of the nectar. Clover honey is well known, but there are many others to try. Two of my favorites are Prairie Sunshine (knapweed honey), a gift from friends in Montana, and macadamia blossom honey, a gift from a friend in Hawaii.

New England's tart, tasty **boiled cider** is apple cider reduced seven times. A choice product, it is available by mail and is often used in custards and pies. (I haven't made my own but it may be worth a try.) Refrigerate the unused portion.

DAIRY PRODUCTS

Grade AA **unsalted butter,** made from sweet cream, is used for all the recipes in this book. Salted butter, which contains approximately 2 percent salt, can be substituted in these recipes; just omit the additional salt called for in the recipe. Whipped butter contains air (to aid spreadability) and should not be used in these recipes. Although butter is recommended, stick **margarine** (not the soft tub kind) can be substituted for butter in these recipes. The cookies will be somewhat different in texture and the flavor will be pleasant, but not quite as good as that of cookies made with butter. **Shortening** wasn't tested in these cookie recipes. If you wish to experiment, note that shortening would be least noticeable in a spicy cookie such as gingerbread and most noticeable in a simple cookie such as shortbread. Store butter and margarine, well covered, in the coldest part of your refrigerator or freeze them. **Cream** is available in supermarkets with varying amounts of butterfat, depending on the brand and category (the minimal butterfat percentage is listed in parentheses): **half-and-half** (10.5 percent), **light cream** (18 percent), **whipping cream** (30 percent), **heavy cream** (36 percent), **Devon double cream** (48 percent), **cream cheese** (33 percent), and **sour cream** (18 percent). Store airtight in the refrigerator. Canned **sweetened condensed milk** (not *evaporated* milk) is concentrated whole milk and sugar.

Grade A large **eggs** were used here. Different-sized eggs will alter the amount of liquid needed in a recipe and results may be skewed. Pay particular attention to the date on the cartons and store them in the refrigerator, in their cardboard container, for maximum freshness.

Meringue powder is a dried egg white product and often substituted for raw egg whites in royal icing, with success. (I've used it many times.) If you make a lot of royal icing, meringue powder earns its keep because its shelf life is much longer than that of fresh eggs and there are no leftover egg yolks. Meringue powder is available by mail and from baking supply stores. It should be stored in a cool, dark place.

CHOCOLATE AND COCOA

South American in origin, cacao beans were used as currency in the New World. In the seventeenth century an exotic beverage made from the beans, named *xocoatl* by the Aztecs and called *chocolate* by the Spaniards, became a royal rage in Europe. Solid chocolate blended with sugar, milk solids, and vanilla is a relatively recent form, only a few hundred years old. Cacao beans begin as white seeds inside large red pods. The tedious process of fermenting, drying, cleaning, roasting, crushing, shelling, grinding, blending, and refining transforms those seeds into chocolate.

Unsweetened chocolate, the purest form, is somewhat bitter and contains no sugar. **Bittersweet chocolate** is slightly sweet. **Semisweet chocolate** is a little sweeter than bittersweet and is the type used in most chips. Both bittersweet and semisweet contain milk solids and vanilla and may be used interchangeably. **Milk chocolate** is the sweetest of all, also containing milk solids and vanilla. **White chocolate** is not really chocolate but sweetened pale yellow cocoa butter with the chocolate solids (liquor) removed. It does contain milk solids, sugar, and vanilla. **Unsweetened cocoa** (not instant cocoa mix) is a powder made of chocolate solids with a little cocoa butter left in. "**Dutch process**" cocoa has had a small amount of alkali added to mellow it.

The taste and quality of chocolate varies tremendously among brands, as the proportion of ingredients has no absolute standard. Taste several brands, side by side, to find your favorite. Both regular and white chocolate are available in bar form (which can be cut into chunks) and chips. White chocolate chips may be called by other names, such as **vanilla milk chips**.

FRUIT AND NUTS

Dried fruit is especially adaptable to baking because of its heightened flavor and low moisture content. I choose naturally dried fruit without additives, if possible. Raisins are tried and true and delicious, of course, but try currants, golden raisins, and Muscat raisins, as well. Dried cherries, cranberries, and blueberries are superb, though not as sweet as raisins. More varieties of dried fruit are becoming available in supermarkets and by mail, or you can dry your own fruit in its prime. Dried figs are storehouses of nutrients and have a distinctive flavor. Dried apricots, apples, pears, and prunes are wonderful additions to cookies.

Dried fruit should be plump and not hardened. Even dried fruit can go so stale that no microwave or hot water bath can revive it. Store in airtight containers in a cool, dark place. Freezing may ruin its texture.

The fragrant peel, or **zest,** of citrus fruit, such as lemon, is often grated and added to cookies for its bright flavor.

Jams, jellies, and preserves are a handy way to use out-of-season, exotic flavors at a moment's notice. (I often shop for new flavors when I travel.) Refrigerate all preserves after opening.

From small pine nuts to large Brazil nuts to even larger coconuts, an enormous array of salubrious **nuts** is used in baking in various forms: slivered, sliced, diced, chopped, ground, pureed (such as peanut butter and almond paste), and whole. Roasting, blanching, and salting give dimensions to flavor. Shelled nuts will turn rancid quickly, so be sure to store them in airtight containers in the refrigerator or freezer. Let them come to room temperature before using.

Seeds, such as sunflower, poppy, and sesame, give crunchy flavor, visual appeal, and nutritional value to cookies. They are best stored in airtight containers in the refrigerator.

Flavorings: Spices, Oils, and Extracts

The fragrance and pungent flavor of spices have been prized for thousands of years. The ancient Greeks and Chinese used spices as healing medicines; the ancient Romans believed that cinnamon was sacred; clove-studded oranges were once thought to ward off the plague during the Middle Ages. The lure of precious spices led to world exploration in the fifteenth and sixteenth centuries and, in turn, to the discovery of America. A treasury of spices is offered at most supermarkets for a fraction of the price they once cost.

Fresh spices have the most intense flavor. Buy a spice grinder if you want to grind your own whole spices. Spices have a shelf life of approximately one year if stored airtight in a cool, dark place. If a spice has lost its fragrance, it's no longer fresh.

Cinnamon, ground from the dried bark of a tropical Asian evergreen tree, is probably the best-liked spice. It has a sweet flavor that, used in small quantity, acts as a flavor enhancer. In larger quantity a spicy flavor results.

Peppery **ginger** is a top-selling spice and traditional in Asian cooking. Ground ginger, made from the dried rhizomes, is the most common form of ginger used in baking. **Crystallized ginger** is fresh ginger that has been simmered in a sugar syrup and dusted with sugar.

Nutmeg and mace are two different spices from one fruit. **Mace** is the outer membrane covering the **nutmeg** shell, dried and ground. Whole nutmeg is the kernel inside the hard, shiny shell (it is usually sold shelled). Nutmeg is easy to grate fresh for a recipe. Use the smallest holes of a regular grater or one of the miniature nutmeg graters (some have a special compartment to hold the nutmeg).

Cloves are the dried, unopened flower buds of the tropical clove tree. Strong in flavor and aroma, this spice is used as a preservative for meats, a component in Asian spice mixtures, and a fragrant addition to gingerbread.

Cardamom, favored by Scandinavian bakers, is the seed of a plant in the ginger family. Whole cardamom seeds are served in some Middle Eastern restaurants to chew and savor, while ground cardamom is an integral ingredient in many savory Middle Eastern dishes.

Allspice is so called because it tastes like a mixture of cinnamon, cloves, and nutmeg. The allspice berry looks like a small peppercorn. Ground, it adds depth to a spice blend.

Pure **vanilla beans** are the fruit pod of an orchid native to Mexico. The most sought-after flavor in the world, vanilla is labor-intensive to produce but actually costs little per recipe and gives big dividends. The complex flavor of vanilla heightens the taste of a wide range of ingredients. The beans contain tiny seeds that add beauty to foods, as well. **Vanilla extract** is the most convenient form of vanilla to use and the variety to choose from is vast. Always use pure vanilla extract, not imitation. Specialty foods stores offer Madagascar, Tahitian, and Mexican vanilla extracts, which have exceptional aromatic flavoring and are a good investment. Try small bottles of different types to choose for yourself. Store vanilla extract tightly capped in a cool, dark place.

In addition to pure vanilla extract, a spectrum of liquid **extracts, essences, flavors, and oils**, is available in supermarkets, specialty foods stores, ethnic markets, baking supply stores, and by mail. They are concentrated forms of natural flavors obtained by distillation and evaporation, extraction, and infusion (imitation flavors exist but aren't recommended). There doesn't seem to be an industry standard, and extracts, essences, and flavors are relatively interchangeable.

Oils are much stronger and should be used sparingly, by the drop. Just the opposite are the larger bottles of flavored *waters*, such as rose water and orange flower water; although these are good products, they are comparatively weak in flavor and not used in these recipes. Store all flavorings tightly capped in a cool, dark place.

DECORATIONS AND FOOD COLORS

Decorating is a creative part of making cookies and is usually done after baking. **Crystallized, or candied, rose petals, violet petals, mimosa, angelica, mint leaves, ginger, lemon peel,** and **orange peel** are the most popular bits of color to put on a cookie with a dab of icing. **Silver dragées** (also known as silver balls) come in different sizes and shapes. Some stores carry dragées in gold, pink, and other colors. Large **sugar crystals,** such as **perlsocker,** and **colored sugar** and **sprinkles** are sprinkled on unbaked cookies or freshly iced cookies. Small **royal icing flowers** may be purchased by the sheet from baking supply stores or made with a special decorating tip. Icing, doughs, and shredded coconut can be tinted. Found in supermarkets, **liquid food coloring** comes in red, yellow, blue, and green, is easy to use, and is suitable for tinting pastel colors. Slightly more expensive (because it's concentrated), **paste food coloring** is the key to intense colors. Paste coloring is available in a range of hues at baking supply stores and by mail; a starter set is a good first choice.

EQUIPMENT

Accurate **measuring spoons and cups** are essential in following recipes for baking. Use the spoons for both liquid and dry ingredients. There are two types of measuring cups: the nested sets of metal or plastic cups (usually in ¼-cup, ⅓-cup, ½-cup, and 1-cup sizes) used to measure dry ingredients, and the heatproof glass measuring cups (available in 1-cup, 2-cup, and 4-cup sizes) used to measure liquids.

A small **kitchen scale**, calibrated from ¼ ounce up to 5 pounds, is enormously useful for weighing chocolate, nuts, and similar ingredients.

A set of three or more nested **mixing bowls** has endless uses and is space efficient.

My honeymoon with the **heavy-duty electric mixer** is not over—even after nine years. I once clung to a small **hand mixer,** but the "hands-free" help of my large mixer won me over. Although any cookie can be mixed by hand, electric mixers (of any size) save much time and energy.

A **food processor** grinds and chops ingredients such as nuts and chocolate in seconds. It also quickly incorporates chunks of cold butter into a dough (optional food processor use is noted in specific recipes). Use the metal blade of the food processor for both procedures. Quality among brands varies; although I use my food processor daily, some are more trouble than help.

A **blender or nut grinder** also may be used to grind nuts. A small coffee grinder may also do the job.

Rubber spatulas are essential for scraping down the sides of a mixing bowl and for removing the last bit of dough. For mixing brownies and cookies by hand, choose a couple of **large wooden spoons** that are comfortable to hold. Don't use wooden spoons with a stiff dough or they may snap in half. Hand washing is recommended. A **plastic dough scraper** cleans dough out of bowls and off work surfaces and rolling pins.

Indispensable **small, medium, and large (balloon) whisks** combine wet or dry mixtures efficiently.

Good-quality sharp **knives** are a key investment in the kitchen. Buy the best. A paring knife, a large chopping knife, and a serrated knife will serve you well over many years. A **pastry wheel** is useful to cut graham crackers, rugelach, and the like. An **X-acto knife** may be used to cut out cookies around a homemade template.

I use dishwasher-proof plastic and wooden **cutting boards** in several sizes. The larger ones are multipurpose. The smallest one is reserved just for cutting garlic, etc. They must be kept immaculately clean or a residue of strong odor can ruin a batch of dough.

A **double boiler** is a two-part pan often used to melt chocolate. The bottom part holds hot or barely simmering water and the top part, fitted in partway, holds the chocolate to be melted. I use another, faster method: my French **porcelain saucepan** (4½ inches in diameter) is used to melt the butter and, off the heat, the chopped chocolate is stirred in. More about melting chocolate is found in "Techniques," page 25.

A large, heavy wooden or marble **rolling pin** rolls out dough quickly and evenly. My professional-sized wooden roller, 15 inches long and 3 inches in diameter, spins while the handles are held stationary. European-style rolling pins have no handles. **Rolling pin thickness guides,** available by mail, or **wooden slats** (mine are custom made) help roll out dough to specific thicknesses. Dough may also be measured with a **ruler,** as well.

A **pastry cloth** is a piece of sturdy woven fabric used to cover a work surface. A **rolling pin cover** is a knitted sleeve that fits over the roller. Lightly floured, these two aids help keep soft dough from sticking while being rolled out.

Although you can use virtually any smooth clean surface to roll out dough, **pastry boards,** available in wood, plastic, and marble, provide a portable, functional work surface, as well. The warm beauty of wood and the dishwasher-safe practicality of plastic make either a good choice. Cool, luxurious marble actually helps keep the butter in pastry from melting during handling.

Small ice cream scoops are a fast way to make uniform drop cookies. I use three sizes: 1¼ inches, 1⅜ inches, and 1¾ inches. Scoops can be cleaned in the dishwasher and are available at gourmet shops and by mail.

Cookie cutters seem to come in infinite variety. Antique cutters are usually made of tin and often have a flat, solid back. (My favorite cutter is an antique bird shape.) On metal cutters, look for sharp, clean edges and smooth seams. Plastic cutters are inexpensive, have no seams, and are most suitable to use with children because they come in bright colors and aren't quite as sharp-edged (and are thus less likely to nick young fingers). Cookie cutters may be found in flea markets, baking supply stores, supermarkets, and by mail. Hand washing is recommended for metal cutters. Many plastic cutters are dishwasher safe, but double-check the manufacturer's instructions, or hand wash to be safe.

A metal or plastic **cookie press** (also called a cookie spritz or cookie gun) comes with many discs and is used to make small decorative cookies. Heavy-gauge metal cookie presses stand up to repeated use, while plastic presses are less expensive but break more easily. Most cookie presses are dishwasher safe. They are available at baking supply stores, some supermarkets, and by mail.

Some **molds** are used to shape cookies *before* baking. They are available in wood, metal, glass, plastic, and unglazed ceramics. Wooden molds are usually lightly floured (or sometimes greased and floured), and other molds are usually very lightly greased, firmly packed with a smooth, stiff dough such as shortbread, then unmolded with a sharp tap onto a baking sheet. Most European and antique molds are wooden and are found in gourmet cooking supply stores. They should be hand washed.

As ovens have different temperatures, an accurate **oven thermometer** will check the heat of your oven so that you can adjust it. A **kitchen timer** is also important.

Use shiny, medium-to heavy-gauge aluminum (a good heat conductor) **baking sheets** with a rim on one side. The rim makes it easier to hold the pan. I prefer regular aluminum sheets to insulated and special-finish pans. Dark baking sheets absorb more heat than shiny, reflective ones and tend to cook cookies too quickly, especially on the bottom. If your baking sheets are too thin (the sheet is very flexible or your cookies burn easily) stack two together and use as one. Good baking sheets are an excellent investment and will last for years.

Choose the largest baking sheet that will fit in your oven, with about 2 inches clearance from the oven walls all around, so that hot air can move freely. If you do a lot of cookie baking, a second or third baking sheet is helpful (one in the oven, one cooling, and one being prepared).

An 8-inch or 9-inch **square pan,** 9- by 13-inch **baking pan**, and 15½-by 10½- by 1-inch **jelly roll pan** are used to bake bar cookies. Either heavy-gauge aluminum or Pyrex baking pans are fine. If you use Pyrex, reduce the oven temperature by 25°. A sturdy pan with a removable bottom (my first choice) allows you to cut bars neatly.

Heavy-gauge aluminum 8-inch and 9-inch **round cake pans or pie pans** can be used for molding or baking shortbread. Some **molded baking pans**, such as madeleine pans, are designed to shape and bake a cookie at the same time. Most special molded pans can be found in gourmet shops and by mail. They are best cleaned by hand with a soft dish-washing brush.

Tartlet pans range in size from 2 to 6 inches and come in all manner of decorative shapes. Tartlets are baked on a baking sheet so they don't fall through the oven racks. Hand washing is easiest.

Pot holders or oven mitts are essential for handling the piping hot baking sheets. A thin-bladed **pancake turner** is an important tool to remove baked cookies from the pans. Two are needed to remove a very large cookie, which should be loosened first with a **long metal spatula**. Use a **small metal spatula** to frost cookies.

A **wire rack** allows cookies to cool quickly. I have a medium rack and an extra-large one. Racks with crisscross wire mesh keep cookies from sliding through better than racks with parallel wires. An old-fashioned method is to let cookies cool on a table, cutting board, or counter covered with a sheet of brown paper (my childhood practice).

Plastic or fabric **pastry bags** (also known as decorating bags), fitted with a coupler to allow **decorative tips** to be changed easily, will attractively pipe icing and soft cookie dough. The tips I use most often are an ⅛-inch round tip and a ½-inch round tip for icing, and small and large star tips for soft dough.

Use a **1-inch pastry brush** to frost or glaze cookies. Mine has natural bristles and a wooden handle, but a brush with a plastic handle with synthetic bristles is okay. Wash it by hand in warm soapy water and let it air dry hanging by the handle. If a wet brush is allowed to dry upside down, the glued portion of the bristles may weaken. Most brushes are not dishwasher safe.

Humble but helpful, inexpensive **waxed paper** is a staple in my home. Introduced in 1927, waxed paper is paraffin-coated tissue paper (triple-waxed). It shouldn't be used to line baking sheets for cookies as the open areas may burn, but it can be used as a pan liner for baking bar cookies, because the waxed paper is completely covered by batter. I also use waxed paper to help roll out stiff doughs (noted in the recipes), to wrap icebox cookies for an old-fashioned look, to line paper bags and boxes to prevent grease marks, to separate layers of cookies to keep them from sticking together, and to slip under cookies being iced.

Baking parchment is a special greaseproof, nonstick paper (usually silicone-coated) that, unlike waxed paper, will withstand direct contact with oven heat. Use it to line baking sheets for sticky cookies that would otherwise bond with the pan. I try to reuse a sheet by placing cookie dough on unused areas. Sold by the roll at supermarkets and by mail, baking parchment is also good for lining cake pans and for cutting into triangles to make disposable pastry bags—a boon when working with children or using many icing colors. The triangles come precut, as well.

Plastic wrap helps to keep cookie dough and icing from drying out and absorbing other flavors in the refrigerator.

Aluminum foil is excellent for lining baking sheets. Aluminum foil also makes for quick cleanup and can be washed and reused.

Heavy **self-sealing plastic bags**, in pint, quart, and gallon sizes, are excellent for storing special flours, nuts, cookies, fruit, leftover icing, and virtually anything that isn't too liquid. It is helpful to label and date the bags.

Cellophane comes made into bags and by the roll to wrap your cookies with sparkle. Both forms are available by mail, party supply stores, and baking supply stores. I always have a stash on hand.

TECHNIQUES

❧ To **test an egg for freshness**, slowly lower it into a tepid glass of water—if it sinks and touches bottom, it's fresh. If it floats, it's not fresh.

❧ To **beat egg whites**, use absolutely clean utensils, beaters, and a bowl without a *trace* of grease or egg yolk that would inhibit volume. A copper bowl may increase volume by chemical reaction to the egg whites. To test for *peaks* dip a spoon into the beaten egg whites and pull it out. If a curved peak results, that is known as a *soft peak*. If a sharp peak results, that is known as a *stiff peak*.

To beat egg whites by hand, place the whites in a large bowl, tilt the bowl at an angle or hold it in the crook of your arm, and whip with a large balloon whisk in a continuous, circular motion. The volume will increase steadily.

To beat egg whites by electric mixer, beat them on high speed, rotating the bowl (or beaters) to reach all of egg whites until the volume has increased significantly.

❧ To **cream butter and sugar** until light and fluffy, combine them on low speed using an electric mixer and increase the speed a bit (unless otherwise indicated in the recipe) until the mixture increases somewhat in volume and becomes lighter in texture and color. This usually just takes a minute or two.

❧ To **beat egg yolks** or whole eggs until pale in color, usually with sugar or a sugar-butter mixture, start on low speed using an electric mixer, slowly increase the speed to medium (unless otherwise indicated in the recipe), and continue beating just until the color of the mixture lightens. This usually happens quickly, in a minute or two.

❧ To **fold in** ingredients, use a large rubber spatula to gently cut and lift through the ingredients in a series of large circular motions. The idea is to deftly combine two mixtures of differing textures, such as beaten egg whites into a dough, without losing the air that was whipped in.

❧ To **knead** dough by hand, place the dough on a lightly floured clean work surface and press in any loose crumbs. Fold the dough in half and gently press together. Rotate the dough a quarter turn and repeat until the dough is smooth.

❧ To make **cookie or graham cracker crumbs**, place the cookies in a heavy self-sealing plastic bag (usually quart sized), press out most of the air, and seal. Roll a heavy rolling pin back and forth to crush the graham crackers. A food processor will also make crumbs, but you will need to break up the cookies first.

❧ To **grind nuts**, place them in a food processor, blender, or coffee grinder and process in short pulses. Don't overprocess or the nuts will turn to nut butter. Special hand-held rotary nut grinders are efficient and inexpensive. **Chop nuts** briefly in a food processor, or on a cutting board using a sharp knife.

❧ To **prepare vanilla sugar**, split a vanilla bean lengthwise and place it in a container filled with about 8 cups of sugar (this doesn't have to be measured) and cover with a tight-fitting lid. Stir the sugar from time to time. I reuse vanilla beans this way after scraping out the tiny seeds for a recipe or simmering the bean in milk for a custard (let it dry first).

❧ To **prepare your own fresh coconut**, choose a heavy coconut sloshing with liquid—an indication of freshness. With an icepick or nail, pierce 2 of the dark eyes and drain the liquid (reserve for another use, if you wish). Wrap the coconut in a dish towel and, with a hammer, crack the coconut into pieces. Or, put the coconut on a baking sheet in a 350°F oven for 15 to 20 minutes, or just until the shell cracks. Wrap the coconut in a dish towel, and, with a hammer, tap it into pieces. Use a spoon to pry the white coconut meat from the shell. Remove the brown skin with a vegetable peeler and grate the coconut by hand or in a food processor.

❧ To **skin hazelnuts**, toast them in a single layer in a shallow pan in a 350°F oven for 10 minutes. Wrap the hot nuts in a clean dish towel, and rub off the skins.

❧ To **melt all types of chocolate**, chop the chocolate and place it in the top part of a double boiler over barely simmering water; stir the chocolate until melted and smooth. A drop of water or steam can stiffen chocolate, so don't let the water heat up too much. Another method is to set a heatproof bowl of chocolate over a saucepan of barely simmering water and stir it until melted. The streamlined method I use, when butter is paired with the chocolate, is to melt the butter in a saucepan (mine is porcelain) over medium heat, then remove the pan from the heat, add the chopped chocolate, and stir until smooth. If all the chocolate doesn't melt, briefly return the pan to very low heat. Another quick method is to melt the chocolate in a microwave, according the manufacturer's directions (usually on brief low heat).

❧ To make **candied citrus peel** (zest), use a sharp vegetable peeler to shave off thin strips of the peel, leaving the white pith, and chop or sliver it. In a medium saucepan, cover the peel with cold water, boil it for 10 minutes, and drain. For each ¼ cup of loosely packed peel, (about 1 orange,) make a sugar syrup by boiling ⅓ cup of sugar and 3 tablespoons of water for 1 minute. Add the peel to the syrup and boil until the peel is translucent, about 15 minutes. Drain the candied peel and spread it out on waxed paper, let it dry, roll it in sugar if you wish, then cover and refrigerate it until ready to use.

❧ To make **royal icing flowers**, fit a Wilton No. 225 or No. 190 tip on a pastry bag. Fill the bag half full with tinted royal icing and twist the top of the bag closed. Firmly hold the bag upright with the tip touching the surface of a sheet of waxed paper or baking parchment and twist your wrist to the left (or right, depending on the tip). Apply pressure to the bag as you untwist to form the flowers; stop the pressure and pull away to finish (it will take a little practice). Stamens made of tiny dots of yellow icing, in the center of each flower, add a little visual punch. Let the icing flowers dry for 24 hours. Peel them off one at a time when ready to use. Freeform flowers can be made with a plain No. 3 tip.

❧ To **soften hardened brown sugar**, place it in a covered container with a cut piece of apple or a slice of bread. Or, use a hammer to pound sugar sealed in a strong freezer bag. Sometimes when there's no alternative I melt the butter in the recipe with the brown sugar over low heat, stirring and breaking up the chunks of sugar until melted, then transfer the mixture to a plate to cool completely, and then use it in the recipe. This will change the recipe somewhat.

TIPS FOR PERFECT COOKIE BAKING

❧ Before baking, read the entire recipe and assemble the ingredients and utensils. That way you won't find something missing mid-recipe.

❧ Use most ingredients near room temperature for proper blending, unless otherwise noted.

❧ Premeasure ingredients such as flour, to prevent being interrupted while counting mid-recipe.

❧ Instead of sifting, dry ingredients may be stirred together thoroughly with a whisk before adding them to the batter. This mixes and aerates the ingredients.

❧ Dry ingredients should be measured by the dip-and-level method: Dip the cup or measuring spoon into the ingredient and level the top with the back of a knife.

❧ Both light brown sugar and dark brown sugar must be firmly packed into a cup when measured for these recipes.

❧ Always measure leavenings accurately using a level, not heaping, measuring spoon. At high altitudes, the amount of leavening may need to be reduced—for the best advice ask local bakers.

❧ Check all liquid measurements in glass measuring cups at eye level.

❧ Use the fewest steps to measure an ingredient. There is less chance of error in measuring ¾ cup of sugar if you use a ½-cup and a ¼-cup measure rather than a ¼-cup measure three times. Some companies include ⅔-cup and ¾-cup measures in a set.

❧ Mix in eggs one at a time, on low speed if using an electric mixer.

❧ Many recipes in this book call for softened butter (especially helpful for hand mixing the dough). Cut the butter into large 1-inch chunks and let it sit at room temperature until somewhat soft to help it cream quickly. A microwave can quickly melt "holes" in butter. I only use it when the butter is frozen—on a very low setting, rotating the butter.

❧ Scrape down the sides of the mixing bowl several times while making batter to ensure that all ingredients are mixed (also scrape dough on mixing spoons and spatulas into the bowl).

❧ Evenly space similarly sized cookies on baking sheets to ensure even baking. The smaller and thinner the cookie, the quicker it bakes. Unless the recipe indicates to keep dough refrigerated, fill any extra baking sheets or sheets of aluminum foil or baking parchment while the first baking sheet is in the oven.

❧ To grease baking sheets, use shortening, not butter or margarine, which may burn. Some recipes will indicate lining the baking sheets with aluminum foil or baking parchment.

❧ Grease pans for bar cookies and molded cookies with shortening, margarine, or butter. Butter can be used here because, unlike a baking sheet, the buttered surface will be covered by dough and won't come in direct contact with heat. I use butter wrappers to grease pans.

Some recipes call for pans to be lightly floured, as well. To do this, place a spoonful of flour in the greased pan. Shake the pan to allow the flour to coat all surfaces. Turn the pan over a sheet of waxed paper and tap out the excess flour.

❧ Bake one sheet of cookies at a time so that hot air can circulate freely. Place the baking sheet on a rack in the center of the oven for even heat distribution. Some ovens have "hot spots." If your cookies tend to brown more quickly in one area, rotate the baking sheet midway through the baking time.

❧ Preheat the oven before baking; it should take about 15 minutes.

❧ Allow an even space between the baking sheet or pan and the oven walls to let heat reach all of the cookies equally.

❧ All cookies spread during baking and some will spread a great deal; chilling the dough helps prevent excess spreading and is called for in some recipes. A minimum spacing guide is given in each recipe, so that the cookies will remain separate.

❧ Baking times are given with each recipe, but oven temperatures, humidity, altitude, and other factors affect the time. I always use a timer set for the minimum time, then test doneness by touching a cookie lightly on top to see if there is any spring to it. Color change is also a clue, but difficult to see in chocolate cookies and brownies. You will often notice an enhanced aroma when the cookies are done.

❧ Let the baking sheet cool between batches, or your cookies will melt before baking. Or, a sheet of aluminum foil or baking parchment, topped with unbaked cookies, can be slid onto a hot baking sheet and immediately baked to shorten the "down time." Foil can be washed and reused.

❧ Before storing, let just-baked cookies cool completely on wire racks, a cool surface, or clean paper—in a single layer.

❧ Store each type of cookie separately, so that flavors don't mingle. For maximum freshness, store cookies in airtight tins, cookie jars, or plastic bags.

❧ Except for custard-type cookies, most cookies will freeze well in a home freezer for up to 1 month. Wrap cookies airtight in plastic wrap or waxed paper, then double wrap them in freezer paper or aluminum foil. Label and date them.

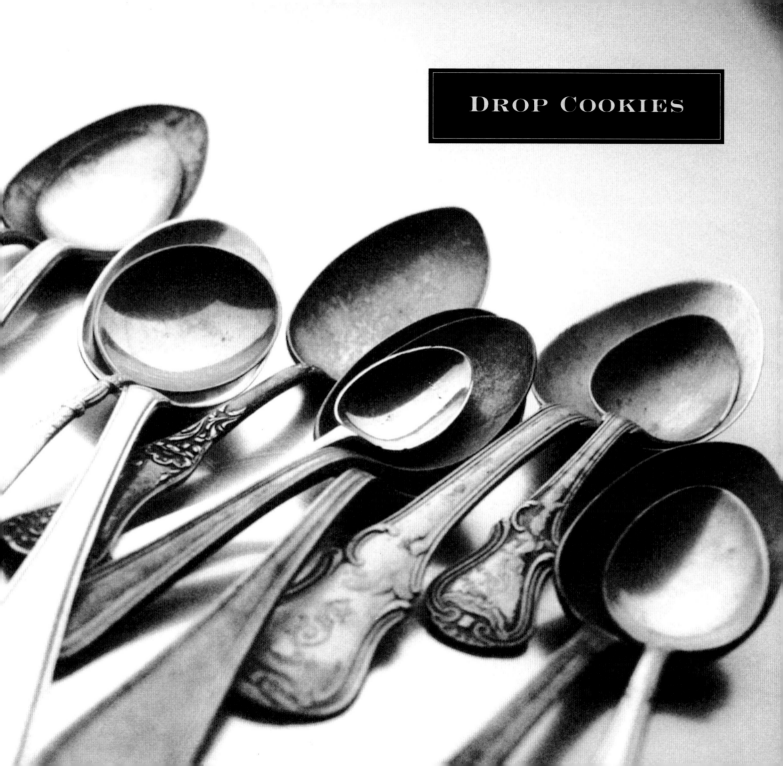

DROP COOKIES

Drop cookies have an appealing handmade look and are made by dropping spoonfuls of soft cookie dough onto baking sheets. Homey chocolate chip cookies, peanut butter cookies, and oatmeal cookies are widely popular drop cookies, but elegant cookies such as Florentines are also made using this technique. This easy-to-do method is good to use with children.

It is important that all the drop cookies on one baking sheet are about the same size so they will bake at the same pace. Try using a small ice cream scoop to shape cookie dough rapidly and uniformly. Two teaspoons work well, too. Use one to scoop a mound of dough, and the other to push off the dough onto the baking sheet.

Before baking, drop cookies can be decoratively flattened with the tines of a fork or the bottom of a glass dipped in sugar to prevent sticking. This will also make the cookie thinner, which will make it bake faster and be crisper.

PRALINE SNAPS

These cookies have a pleasing crispness and a buttery praline flavor. The oats are quickly ground in a blender or a food processor.

2 cups all-purpose flour
½ teaspoon salt
1 teaspoon baking powder
¼ teaspoon baking soda
1½ cups old-fashioned or quick (not instant) rolled oats, coarsely ground
1 cup plus 2 tablespoons (2¼ sticks) unsalted butter, softened
1½ cups firmly packed dark brown sugar
1½ teaspoons pure vanilla extract

Preheat the oven to 350°F. In a medium bowl, stir together the flour, salt, baking powder, baking soda, and oats; set aside. In a large bowl, using an electric mixer on medium speed, cream the butter and sugar. Add the vanilla extract. On low speed, gradually add the flour mixture and combine well. ¶Scoop the dough into 1¼-inch balls and place 2 inches apart on ungreased baking sheets. Flatten the balls slightly with the bottom of a glass. ¶Bake in the center of the oven for about 12 minutes, or until barely browned around the edges. Let the cookies cool on the baking sheet for a few minutes, then transfer them to a wire rack to cool completely. Store in an airtight container. Well-wrapped cookies may be frozen.

Makes about 4 dozen cookies

BLACK TREACLE TEA CAKES

These tea cakes are reminiscent of parkin, a delicious English gingerbread made with oats. Black treacle is a faintly sulfured cane syrup, darker, thicker, and less sweet than mild, unsulfured American molasses. I discovered black treacle when I lived in London and grew to enjoy its smoky, bold flavor. The formula has changed a bit fairly recently, according to Tate & Lyle (the key producers of black treacle), and it seems a little stronger now, so I use one part American unsulfured molasses to two parts treacle to obtain the flavor I like. Black treacle is found in specialty foods stores and by mail. These cookies are best the day after they are baked.

2⅔ cups all-purpose flour
¼ cup old-fashioned or quick (not instant) rolled oats
½ teaspoon baking soda
½ teaspoon salt
2½ teaspoons ground ginger
1¼ teaspoons ground cinnamon
¼ teaspoon ground allspice
½ cup (1 stick) unsalted butter, softened
¾ cup sugar
2 large eggs
½ cup black treacle or unsulfured molasses
¼ cup unsulfured molasses
⅔ cup milk (decrease milk to ½ cup if using all molasses)
Treacle Cream Filling (recipe follows)

Preheat the oven to 375°F. Grease and lightly flour the baking sheets. In a medium bowl, whisk together the flour, oats, baking soda, salt, ginger, cinnamon, and allspice; set aside. In a large bowl, using an electric mixer on medium speed, cream the butter and sugar together until fluffy. Beat in the eggs, one at a time. Mix in the treacle and/or molasses. On low speed, add about one third of the flour mixture at a time, alternately with the milk, mixing until blended. ¶Drop teaspoonfuls of dough 2 inches apart on the baking sheets. Bake in the center of the oven for about 12 minutes, or until a cookie springs back when lightly touched (like a baked cake). Let the cookies cool on the baking sheet for a few minutes, then transfer to a wire rack to cool completely. ¶Prepare the treacle cream filling. Spread a ¼-inch layer of filling on the bottom side of a cookie and top immediately with a similarly sized cookie, with the bottom side touching the filling. Repeat with the remaining cookies. Wrap cookies individually in plastic wrap if you plan to store them in layers or travel with them, because they tend to cling together. Well-wrapped cookies may be frozen.

Treacle Cream Filling

½ cup (1 stick) unsalted butter, softened
2 cups confectioners' sugar, sifted
½ teaspoon ground ginger
¼ cup black treacle or unsulfured molasses
¼ teaspoon salt
2 to 3 tablespoons milk

In a medium bowl, with an electric mixer on low speed, cream the butter and confectioners' sugar together. Add the ginger, treacle or molasses, salt, and 2 tablespoons milk and beat on low speed until smooth and creamy. Add the remaining milk a teaspoonful at a time until the mixture seems easily spreadable.

Makes about 3 dozen sandwich cookies

Chewy Molasses Cookies

Spices permeate these large, homey cookies. Unlike gingersnaps, these cookies are smooth and chewy, especially if not overbaked. They perfume the kitchen with the sweet scent of spice when they bake.

2¾ *cups all-purpose flour*
1 *teaspoon baking soda*
½ *teaspoon salt*
1½ *teaspoons ground ginger*
1 *teaspoon ground cinnamon*
½ *teaspoon ground nutmeg*
½ *teaspoon ground allspice*
¼ *teaspoon ground cloves*
¾ *cup firmly packed dark brown sugar*
¾ *cup (1½ sticks) unsalted butter, softened*
1 *large egg*
¾ *cup unsulfured molasses*

Preheat the oven to 350°F. Grease the baking sheets. In a medium bowl, whisk together the flour, baking soda, salt, ginger, cinnamon, nutmeg, allspice, and cloves; set aside. In a large bowl, with an electric mixer on medium speed, cream the brown sugar and butter together. Add the egg and molasses, and beat until light colored and creamy. On low speed, gradually add the flour mixture. ¶Drop heaping tablespoonfuls of dough (or use a 1¾-inch scoop) 3 inches apart on the baking sheets. Bake in the center of the oven for about 10 to 15 minutes, or until set but not browned. Let the cookies cool on the baking sheet for a few minutes, then transfer them to a wire rack to cool completely. Store in an airtight container. Well-wrapped cookies may be frozen.

Makes about 1 dozen large cookies

Amaretti

There are several ways to make this type of Italian almond meringue cookie. Some recipes call for mixtures to be partially cooked in a skillet and others require stiffly beaten egg whites. This recipe is very easy and very good. The cookies can be sandwiched together with jam or melted chocolate and festively wrapped in colored waxed paper squares (whole sheets are available by mail). Amaretti are a nice to serve with espresso.

1 *cup (10 ounces) almond paste, cut into ¼-inch slices*
⅓ *cup sugar*
2 *large egg whites*
1 *teaspoon pure vanilla extract*
18 *to 24 almond slivers (optional)*

Preheat the oven to 350°F. Line the baking sheets with baking parchment. In a medium bowl, with an electric mixer on low speed, combine the almond paste and sugar. Blend in the egg whites and vanilla extract. ¶Pipe or drop teaspoonfuls of dough 1½ inches apart on the prepared baking sheets. Decorate each cookie with an almond sliver, if you like. ¶Bake in the center of the oven for about 15 to 20 minutes, or until golden. Let the cookies cool completely before removing them from the baking sheet. Store in an airtight container. Well-wrapped cookies may be frozen.

Makes about 20 cookies

COCONUT MACAROONS

These are the irresistible macaroons my mother used to make. When my family lived in Puerto Rico, my father would hack coconuts open with a machete right through the large fibrous outer husk to the hard brown inner shell, and the fresh coconut meat was delightful. If you wish to prepare fresh coconut, see page 25.

⅓ cup all-purpose flour
¾ cup sweetened condensed milk (not evaporated)
1 teaspoon pure vanilla extract
¼ teaspoon ground cinnamon
¼ teaspoon salt
3 cups (about 8½ ounces) shredded coconut

Preheat the oven to 350°F. Line the baking sheets with baking parchment. In a large bowl, with a large wooden spoon, combine the flour, sweetened condensed milk, vanilla extract, cinnamon, and salt. Stir in the coconut, coating it well with the batter. ¶ Drop rounded teaspoonfuls of dough (or use a 1¼-inch scoop) 2 inches apart on the baking sheets. Bake in the center of the oven for about 15 minutes, or until nicely browned at the edges. Let the cookies cool on the baking sheet for a few minutes, then transfer them to a wire rack to cool completely. Store in an airtight container.

Makes about 2½ dozen cookies

ORANGE ALMOND WEDDING CAKES

This type of cookie is known by other names—bride's cakes, Mexican wedding cakes, Russian tea cakes—but these cookies have the orange-almond flavor sometimes used in wedding cakes. They also have an elegant orange glaze and an optional decoration, such as a royal icing flower, an almond slice, or a silver dragée. A time-consuming but lovely decoration is a small bow formed from a sliver of orange zest. These cookies are simple to make, making them a good choice to produce on a large scale (a final dusting of confectioners' sugar instead of the orange icing would be quick to do). The recipe may be doubled.

2 cups all-purpose flour
¼ teaspoon salt
1 cup (2 sticks) unsalted butter, softened
½ cup confectioners' sugar, sifted
1 tablespoon grated orange zest, or 1 teaspoon orange extract
1 teaspoon pure vanilla extract
½ teaspoon pure almond extract
1 cup (5 ounces) almonds, finely chopped
Orange Icing (recipe follows) and decoration of choice

Preheat the oven to 325°F. Grease the baking sheets. In a small bowl, whisk together the flour and salt; set aside. In a large bowl, with an electric mixer on low speed, cream the butter and confectioners' sugar together until pale in color. Add the orange zest or extract, vanilla extract, and almond extract. Gradually beat the flour mixture into the butter mixture. Stir in the chopped almonds. Roll the dough into 1¼-inch balls in the palms of your hands. Place the balls 2 inches apart on the baking sheets. ¶Bake in the center of the oven for about 10 to 12 minutes, or until set but not browned. Let the cookies cool on

the baking sheet for a few minutes, then carefully transfer them to a wire rack to cool completely. ¶Make the orange icing. Glaze the cookies, using a pastry brush to "paint" the cookies with icing, and immediately top with a tiny decoration, if you like. Store in an airtight container, preferably in a single layer or between sheets of waxed paper. Unfrosted cookies will freeze well.

Makes about 3 dozen cookies

Orange Icing
1⅓ *cups confectioners' sugar, sifted*
2 *tablespoons orange juice or Grand Marnier*
A tiny dot of orange food coloring (optional)

In a small bowl, whisk all the ingredients together. If the icing seems too thick, add a few drops more of orange juice. Cover with plastic wrap touching the surface of the icing (to prevent a crust forming). This icing may be made several hours ahead.

Summer Citrus Wafers

The clean, fresh flavor of citrus is delectable in these crisp wafers. I love to serve them in warm weather with a tall glass of iced tea. Although the dough is soft enough to pipe into attractive cookies using a pastry bag, it also may be used to make simple drop cookies.

½ *cup (1 stick) unsalted butter, softened*
½ *cup sugar*
1 *large egg white*
⅛ *teaspoon salt*
1 *teaspoon grated lemon zest*
1 *teaspoon grated orange zest*
1 *teaspoon vanilla*
⅔ *cup all-purpose flour*

Preheat the oven to 350°F. In a medium bowl, with an electric mixer on medium speed, cream the butter and sugar together. Mix in the egg white, salt, lemon zest, orange zest, and the vanilla. On low speed, add the flour and mix well. ¶Drop rounded teaspoonfuls of dough 3 inches apart on ungreased baking sheets. The cookies will spread. Or, transfer the dough to a pastry bag fitted with a ½-inch round tip, and pipe cookies 3 inches apart on the baking sheets. ¶Bake in the center of the oven for about 12 to 15 minutes, or until the wafers are nicely brown around the edges. Let the cookies cool on the baking sheet for a few minutes, then transfer them to a wire rack to cool completely. Store in an airtight container. Well-wrapped cookies may be frozen.

Makes about 2 dozen cookies

Banana-Orange Coconut Cookies

The tropical trio of banana, orange, and coconut results in an ambrosial cookie. Just before baking, the cookies are sprinkled with coconut, which toasts to a golden hue. If you wish, you can prepare fresh coconut using the directions on page 25.

1¾ cups all-purpose flour
½ teaspoon baking powder
½ teaspoon baking soda
½ teaspoon salt
⅛ teaspoon ground cinnamon
¾ cup (1½ sticks) unsalted butter, softened
½ cup firmly packed light brown sugar
⅓ cup granulated sugar
1 large egg
1 tablespoon grated orange zest
½ teaspoon pure vanilla extract
¼ cup orange juice, preferably fresh
1 medium banana, mashed (about ½ cup)
1½ cups (about 4½ ounces) shredded coconut, divided

Preheat the oven to 350°F. Grease the baking sheets. In a medium bowl, whisk together the flour, baking powder, baking soda, salt, and cinnamon; set aside. In a large bowl, with an electric mixer on medium speed, cream the butter, brown sugar, and sugar together. On low speed, add the egg, orange zest, vanilla extract, orange juice, and banana; beat until smooth. Add the flour mixture to the butter mixture. Stir in 1¼ cups of the coconut. ¶Drop rounded tablespoonfuls of dough (or use a 1¼-inch scoop) 2 inches apart on the baking sheets. Sprinkle tops of cookies with the reserved coconut. Bake in the center of the oven for about 12 to 14 minutes, or until the cookies are very light brown and some of the coconut on top has toasted. Let the cookies cool on the baking sheet for a few minutes, then transfer them to a wire rack to cool completely. Store in an airtight container.

Makes about 3 dozen cookies

MERINGUE KISSES

Meringue kisses are cholesterol-free crunchy confections that are more candy than cookie. This is a good recipe to use when extra egg whites are on hand and are best made on a cool, dry day. In the summertime I serve large meringues filled with vanilla ice cream, topped with pureed fresh berries, with a few whole berries as garnish.

3 large egg whites
½ teaspoon cream of tartar
⅛ teaspoon salt
½ cup superfine sugar
1 teaspoon pure vanilla extract

Preheat the oven to 200°F. Line the baking sheets with baking parchment. In a large bowl, with an electric mixer on low speed, mix the egg whites, cream of tartar, and salt. Increase the speed to high and beat the egg whites until they start to thicken. Gradually add the sugar in a stream while beating the mixture. Add the vanilla extract and beat until stiff peaks form. ¶Fill a large pastry bag fitted with a ½-inch star tip half full with the meringue mixture and twist the top of the bag closed. Pipe the meringue into 1 inch mounds, 1½ inches apart on the baking sheet. ¶Bake in the center of the oven for about 1 hour, or until meringues are set and just begin to change color. When completely cool, remove the cookies from the baking sheet with a spatula or pancake turner. Store in an airtight container.

Makes about 2 dozen cookies

HAZELNUT THINS

Hazelnuts, also known as filberts, are popular in European baked goods and are becoming more popular here. These elegant, crisp cookies are quick to make and perfect for topping parfaits or serving with coffee. Unskinned hazelnuts were used here for extra flavor, but skinned nuts are also fine. A dash of Frangelico liqueur may be used to heighten the cookie's hazelnut flavor.

2 large egg whites
½ cup sugar
1 cup (5 ounces) hazelnuts, coarsely ground
¼ teaspoon salt
1 teaspoon Frangelico liqueur or vanilla extract

Preheat the oven to 325°F. Line the baking sheets with baking parchment or aluminum foil. In a medium bowl, whisk the egg whites and sugar together just to combine. Add the hazelnuts, salt, and Frangelico liqueur or vanilla extract, blending well. ¶Drop teaspoonfuls of dough 3 inches apart onto the prepared baking sheets. Bake in the center of the oven for about 15 minutes, or until light brown around the edges. Let the cookies cool on the baking sheet for a few minutes, then transfer them to a wire rack to cool completely. Store in an airtight container. Well-wrapped cookies may be frozen.

Makes about 1½ dozen cookies

PECAN LACE

Ground pecans, bound with a soft batter, spread greatly during baking to form beautifully filigreed, crisp cookies. Virtually any kind of nut can be used, and each variety will produce a slightly different texture. Sandwich the cookies with ganache, a delicious chocolate cream that is surprisingly easy to make.

4 tablespoons (½ stick) unsalted butter
½ cup sugar
2 tablespoons all-purpose flour
½ teaspoon salt
2 tablespoons heavy cream
1 cup (4 ounces) pecans, ground
Ganache (recipe follows)

Preheat the oven to 350°F. Grease and flour the baking sheets, or line them with aluminum foil or baking parchment. In a medium saucepan over medium heat, melt the butter and set aside. In a medium bowl, stir together the sugar, flour, and salt; add the melted butter. Blend in the cream and pecans. The dough will be very soft. ¶Drop scant teaspoonfuls of dough 3 inches apart on the prepared baking sheets. Bake in the center of the oven for about 7 to 10 minutes, or until the cookies are light brown around the edges and golden on top. Do not underbake. Let the cookies cool completely on the baking sheet before removing. ¶Make the ganache. Spread a ⅛-inch layer of the ganache on the flat bottom of a cookie. Top with another cookie, with the flat side touching the filling. Repeat with the remaining cookies and ganache. Store in an airtight container.

Makes about 2 dozen cookie sandwiches

Ganache

½ *cup heavy cream*

5 *squares (5 ounces) semisweet chocolate, chopped*

1 *teaspoon Cognac or pure vanilla extract*

In a small saucepan, bring the cream to a boil. Remove from the heat, add the chocolate. Whisk until the chocolate is melted and cooled to lukewarm. Stir in the Cognac or vanilla extract.

FLORENTINES

These festive, candylike almond wafers are studded with dots of candied orange peel (if you wish to make your own, see page 25) and have a chocolate undercoating. Traditionally, the chocolate is marked with decorative wavy lines just before it sets. These are best made on a cool, dry day. Florentines would be good to serve at an elegant tea or to give as a luxurious gift.

1 *cup (4 ounces) sliced almonds, divided*

3 *tablespoons unsalted butter*

⅓ *cup sugar*

¼ *cup all-purpose flour*

⅛ *teaspoon salt*

2 *tablespoons honey*

2 *tablespoons heavy cream*

⅓ *cup minced candied orange peel*

¼ *teaspoon pure almond extract*

3 *drops orange oil (optional)*

Chocolate Undercoating (recipe follows)

Preheat the oven to 350°F. Line the baking sheets with aluminum foil and grease the foil. Finely chop ½ cup of the almonds by hand or in a food processor. In a heavy, medium saucepan, melt the butter over medium heat. When the foam subsides, whisk in the sugar. Add the flour and salt. Blend in the honey and cream and bring to a low boil. Reduce the heat and simmer for 2 minutes. Remove from the heat and stir in the sliced and chopped almonds and candied orange peel. Stir in the almond extract and orange oil. ¶Drop level teaspoonfuls of dough 3 inches apart on the prepared baking sheets. Bake in the center of the oven for about 8 to 9 minutes, or until the cookies have medium brown edges and are still light brown in the center. Once they start browning, they'll darken quickly. Let the cookies cool on the baking sheet for a few minutes, then transfer them to a wire rack to cool completely. ¶Make the chocolate undercoating. Use a spatula to coat the bottom of each cookie with the chocolate (some chocolate will ooze through, which I find appealing). When the chocolate is about to set (the length of time will vary depending on weather conditions), draw the tines of a fork or a pastry comb through the undercoating to score the traditional wavy lines (this may take practice). Let the cookies sit until the chocolate has set (refrigerate to speed this up). Store in an airtight container between sheets of waxed paper.

Makes about 3½ dozen wafers

Chocolate Undercoating

1 *tablespoon unsalted butter*

6 *ounces semisweet chocolate, chopped*

Melt the butter and chocolate in the top of a double boiler over barely simmering water, stirring until smooth. Let the chocolate cool to lukewarm before using.

Variation: For fancy Florentines, instead of scoring the chocolate undercoating decorate it with pieces of nuts, bits of candied fruit, and a few currants pushed into the chocolate before it sets (this is now the top of the cookie).

BENNE WAFERS

The benne (pronounced "benny") wafer is a sesame seed cookie traditional in the South since colonial days. According to legend, the seeds bring good luck to those who eat them. These unique cookies are perfect to make in miniature to serve at a party.

½ cup white sesame seeds
¾ cup all-purpose flour
¼ teaspoon salt
¼ teaspoon baking powder
½ cup (1 stick) unsalted butter, softened
1 cup firmly packed light brown sugar
1 large egg
1½ teaspoons pure vanilla extract

In a dry skillet over medium heat, stir the sesame seeds for about 10 minutes, or until lightly toasted. Pour into a bowl to cool. Preheat the oven to 350°F. Line the baking sheets with aluminum foil. In a small bowl, whisk together the flour, salt, and baking powder; set aside. In a medium bowl, use a large wooden spoon to cream the butter and brown sugar together. Mix in the egg and vanilla extract. Add the flour mixture to the batter. Stir in the cooled sesame seeds. ¶Drop rounded teaspoonfuls of dough 3 inches apart on the baking sheets (these cookies will spread a great deal). Bake in the center of the oven for about 10 minutes, or until evenly browned. Let the cookies cool on the baking sheet for a few minutes. Slide the whole sheet of foil to a wire rack to cool completely before removing the cookies, or they will stick to the foil. Store in an airtight container. Well-wrapped cookies (separated with sheets of waxed paper to prevent sticking together) may be frozen.

Makes about 3 dozen medium-large wafers

CHOCOLATE CHUNK COOKIES

The familiar semisweet chocolate chips in America's favorite cookie may be replaced with chunks of gourmet chocolate chopped from a solid bar. My friends and family are evenly divided on the inclusion of nuts, so I often bake half the dough without nuts and add half (or sometimes even *all*) of the nuts called for in the recipe to the remaining dough.

2⅓ cups all-purpose flour
1 teaspoon baking soda
1 teaspoon salt
1 cup (2 sticks) unsalted butter, softened
1 cup firmly packed light brown sugar
¼ cup sugar
2 large eggs
2 teaspoons pure vanilla extract
12 ounces chocolate, chopped into chunks
   or 2 cups (12 ounces) chocolate chips
1¾ cup (7 ounces) pecans or walnuts, chopped

Preheat the oven to 350° F. In a small bowl, whisk together the flour, baking soda, and salt; set aside. In a large bowl, with an electric mixer on medium speed, cream together the butter, brown sugar, and sugar until fluffy. Mix in the eggs and vanilla extract. On low speed, gradually beat in the flour mixture. Stir in the chocolate chunks and nuts. ¶Drop rounded teaspoonfuls of dough 2 inches apart on ungreased baking sheets. Bake in the center of the oven for about 9 to 10 minutes, or until just set but not browned. Let the cookies cool on the baking sheet for a few minutes, then transfer them to a wire rack to cool completely. Store in an airtight container. Well-wrapped cookies may be frozen.

Makes about 3 dozen cookies

PEANUT BUTTER COOKIES

There is a luxurious amount of peanut butter in these classic American cookies. I've tested all kinds of peanut butter in this recipe—natural foods brands, various supermarket brands, and even homemade—and found that a national brand using just ground peanuts and salt made the best-tasting cookie with a tender texture. The cinnamon acts as a flavor enhancer.

2¼ cups all-purpose flour
1 teaspoon baking soda
¼ teaspoon ground cinnamon
½ teaspoon salt
2 cups creamy peanut butter
1 cup (2 sticks) unsalted butter, softened
1¾ cups firmly packed dark brown sugar
2 large eggs
2 teaspoons pure vanilla extract

Preheat the oven to 375°F. In a small bowl, whisk together the flour, baking soda, cinnamon, and salt; set aside. In a large bowl, with an electric mixer on low speed, cream together the peanut butter, butter, and brown sugar. Beat in the eggs and vanilla extract. Slowly add the flour mixture and mix well. ¶Drop rounded teaspoonfuls of dough (or use a 1¼-inch scoop) 2 inches apart on ungreased baking sheets. Gently press the tines of a fork across the top of each cookie to form the traditional crisscross mark of the All-American peanut butter cookie. The thickness of the cookie will be affected by the pressure used with the fork. Heavy pressure will produce a thin, crisp cookie, and light pressure will produce a thick, soft cookie (baking time affects crispness, as well). If the fork sticks, lightly flour it. ¶Bake in the center of the oven for about 8 to 10 minutes, or until set but not browned. Let the cookies cool on the baking sheet for a few minutes, then transfer them to a wire rack to cool completely. Store in an airtight container. Well-wrapped cookies may be frozen.

Makes about 4½ dozen cookies

WHITE CHOCOLATE MACADAMIA COOKIES

The wildly popular macadamia nut was named after Dr. John McAdam, a friend of the Australian scientist who first described the nuts botanically. Here they are paired with white chocolate to make cookies that cause special requests.

1½ cups all-purpose flour
½ teaspoon baking soda
¼ teaspoon salt
¾ cup (1½ sticks) unsalted butter, softened
½ cup firmly packed light brown sugar
¼ cup sugar
1 large egg
1½ teaspoons pure vanilla extract
6 ounces white chocolate, chopped, or 1 cup vanilla milk chips
½ cup (2½ ounces) macadamia nuts (salted or unsalted), coarsely chopped

Preheat the oven to 350° F. In a medium bowl, whisk together the flour, baking soda, and salt; set aside. In a large bowl, with an electric mixer on medium speed, cream the butter, brown sugar, and sugar together. Add the egg and vanilla extract. On low speed, add the flour mixture. By hand, stir in the white chocolate or vanilla milk chips and macadamia nuts. ¶Drop rounded tablespoonfuls of dough 2 inches apart on ungreased baking sheets. Bake in the center of the oven for about 9 to 12 minutes, or just until set but not browned. Let the cookies cool on the baking sheet for a few minutes, then transfer them to a wire rack to cool completely. Store in an airtight container. Well-wrapped cookies may be frozen.

Makes about 1½ dozen cookies

DOUBLE FUDGE DROPS

An indulgence for chocolate aficionados: a soft, dark chocolate cookie chock-full of bittersweet chocolate chunks that is as good as it sounds. Choose premium-quality chocolate for these cookies.

¼ cup all-purpose flour
⅛ teaspoon baking powder
¼ teaspoon salt
4 tablespoons (½ stick) unsalted butter
7 squares (7 ounces) bittersweet or semisweet chocolate, chopped, divided
1 large egg
½ cup sugar
1 teaspoon pure vanilla extract

Preheat the oven to 350° F. Line the baking sheets with baking parchment or aluminum foil. Chop 4 squares of the chocolate coarsely and set aside. Chop the remaining 3 squares of chocolate into smaller chunks and set aside. In a small bowl, whisk together the flour, baking powder, and salt; set aside. ¶In the top of a double boiler set over barely simmering water, melt the butter and coarsely chopped chocolate, stirring until smooth. Set aside to cool for a few minutes. In a medium bowl, whisk together the egg and sugar; add the vanilla extract. Whisk in the melted chocolate mixture. Gradually add the flour mixture to the batter. Stir in the smaller chocolate chunks. ¶Drop rounded teaspoonfuls of dough 2 inches apart on the prepared baking sheets. Bake in the center of the oven for about 13 to 15 minutes, or until glossy and set. Let the cookies cool on the baking sheet for a few minutes, then transfer them to a wire rack to cool completely. Store in an airtight container. Well-wrapped cookies may be frozen.

Makes about 1½ dozen cookies

RAIN FOREST DROPS

In honor of the Brazilian rain forest, this tender mocha java cookie is loaded with Brazil nuts. When I was a child, my father brought home a large pod of Brazil nuts from his trip to Rio de Janeiro. The top half of the pod was artistically carved away to expose the nuts nestled beautifully inside.

1½ cups all-purpose flour
¾ teaspoon baking soda
½ teaspoon salt
¼ teaspoon ground cinnamon
2 squares (2 ounces) semisweet chocolate, chopped
4 teaspoons instant coffee granules
1½ teaspoons hot water
½ cup (1 stick) unsalted butter, softened
½ cup sugar
⅓ cup firmly packed dark brown sugar
1 large egg
½ cup (2½ ounces) Brazil nuts, chopped

Preheat the oven to 350°F. In a small bowl, whisk together the flour, baking soda, salt, and cinnamon; set aside. In the top of a double boiler over barely simmering water, melt the chocolate, stirring until smooth. Set the chocolate aside to cool slightly. ¶ In a cup, dissolve the instant coffee in the hot water. In a large bowl, with an electric mixer on low speed, beat the coffee, butter, sugar, and brown sugar until creamy. Add the egg and melted chocolate. Gradually beat the flour mixture into the chocolate mixture. Stir in the Brazil nuts. ¶ Drop rounded tablespoonfuls of dough 2 inches apart on ungreased baking sheets. Bake in the center of the oven for about 10 to 12 minutes, or until set but not browned. Let the cookies cool on the baking sheet for a few minutes, then transfer them to a wire rack to cool completely. Store in an airtight container. Well-wrapped cookies may be frozen.

Makes about 3 dozen cookies

PEANUT BUTTER OATMEAL COOKIES

Packed with peanut butter and oatmeal, two flavors children love, these cookies will be a lunch box favorite. The recipe may be doubled.

1 cup all-purpose flour
1 cup old-fashioned or quick (not instant) rolled oats
½ teaspoon baking soda
¼ teaspoon ground cinnamon
¼ teaspoon salt
½ cup (1 stick) unsalted butter, softened
1 cup firmly packed light brown sugar
1 cup creamy peanut butter
1 large egg
1 teaspoon pure vanilla extract

Preheat the oven to 325°F. In a medium bowl, whisk together the flour, oats, baking soda, cinnamon, and salt; set aside. In a large bowl, with an electric mixer on medium speed, beat together the butter, brown sugar, and peanut butter until creamy. Beat in the egg and vanilla extract. On low speed, add the flour mixture mixing just until blended. ¶ Drop rounded teaspoonfuls of dough 2 inches apart onto ungreased baking sheets. Bake in the center of the oven for about 10 to 12 minutes, or until set but not browned. Let the cookies cool on the baking sheet for a few minutes, then transfer them to a wire rack to cool completely. Store in an airtight container. Well-wrapped cookies may be frozen.

Makes about 3 dozen cookies

BLUEBERRY OATMEAL COOKIES

Oatmeal cookies, another American favorite, traditionally have raisins, but you can give them new flavor with dried blueberries, cherries, or cranberries. Look for these dried fruits in natural foods stores and specialty foods stores or order them by mail.

¾ cup all-purpose flour
1½ cups old-fashioned or quick (not instant) rolled oats
½ teaspoon baking soda
¼ teaspoon salt
½ cup (1 stick) unsalted butter, softened
1 cup firmly packed light brown sugar
1 large egg
1 tablespoon milk or water
½ teaspoon pure almond or vanilla extract
½ cup dried blueberries, cherries, cranberries, or raisins
⅓ cup (1 ounce) sliced almonds

Preheat the oven to 350° F. In a medium bowl, whisk together the flour, oats, baking soda, and salt; set aside. In a large bowl, with an electric mixer on medium speed, cream the butter and brown sugar together. Blend in the egg, milk, and almond or vanilla extract. On low speed, blend in the flour mixture. By hand, stir in the dried fruit and almonds. ¶Drop rounded teaspoonfuls of dough 2 inches apart on ungreased baking sheets. Bake in the center of the oven for about 12 to 14 minutes, or until the edges start to brown. Let the cookies cool on the baking sheet for a few minutes, then transfer them to a wire rack to cool completely. Store in an airtight container. Well-wrapped cookies may be frozen.

Makes about 2½ dozen cookies

BAR COOKIES

Of the five basic types of cookies in this book, bars are usually the quickest to prepare. One-layer bars, such as brownies, are speedy to make because, once the dough is mixed, it is simply spread into a baking pan and popped into the oven. Bars can be baked in several layers as well. Often a layer of dough will be spread into a baking pan and partially baked into a firm crust, then a liquid layer added and baked into a custard.

For picnics and casual outdoor parties, it is hard to beat the convenience of serving the cookies right from the pan. The sturdy nature of firm bars also make them good for mailing. Novelty-shaped pans, such as a heart or dinosaur, can also be used to bake the bars, thus adding to the presentation without adding to the preparation time. The pan should be similar in size to the one suggested in the recipe so that the baking time will be about the same. Give special attention to the physical signs of doneness mentioned in every recipe, always the best indication.

Bars can be cut into squares, rectangles, diamonds, triangles, and fingers. One-layer bars can also be cut into decorative shapes with cookie cutters. Don't worry—there is usually a volunteer to eat the crumbs.

GUAVA COCONUT DREAM BARS

Being raised in a military family, I moved every two or three years and enjoyed the perquisite of sampling foreign foods. Tasting coconuts and guavas was part of my initiation into the tropics. Guava jam is much easier to find than the fruit and is a delicious partner to coconut. Directions for preparing fresh coconut are on page 25, if you'd like to give it a try.

¾ *cup (1½ sticks) unsalted butter, softened*
⅓ *cup sugar*
1¼ *teaspoons pure vanilla extract*
1½ *cups all-purpose flour*
½ *teaspoon salt*
⅞ *cup guava jam*
¾ *cup (2¼ ounces) shredded coconut*
¼ *cup (1 ounce) pecans, chopped*

Preheat the oven to 350° F. Grease an 8-inch square baking pan. In a medium bowl, with an electric mixer on low speed, mix together the butter, sugar, vanilla, flour, and salt until well combined and crumbly. ¶Reserve ¾ cup of the mixture. Firmly press the remaining dough into the bottom of the pan. ¶Bake in the center of the oven for about 15 to 18 minutes or until lightly browned. Carefully spread the jam evenly over the hot crust. Combine the reserved crumb mixture, coconut, and pecans, and sprinkle over the jam. Bake in the center of the oven for about 25 minutes, or until the top is golden brown. Let cool completely before cutting into bars. Store in an airtight container.

Makes 16 bars

ALMOND APRICOT BARS

Dried apricots are used in these superb bars. They have a tender shortbread crust and a moist, beautifully colored apricot cream layer topped with sliced almonds. The bars are rich and should be cut into small bars or triangles.

¾ cup dried apricots

1 cup all-purpose flour

1 cup plus 3 tablespoons sugar, divided

¼ teaspoon salt

½ cup (1 stick) cold unsalted butter, cut into ¼-inch pieces

1 large egg

2 tablespoons orange juice

3 ounces cream cheese, softened and quartered

⅓ cup (1 ounce) sliced almonds

Preheat the oven to 350° F. Lightly grease an 8-inch square baking pan. Place the apricots in a small bowl and pour boiling water over them to cover. Let soak for 10 minutes. ¶Meanwhile, in a food processor, pulse together the flour, 3 tablespoons sugar, and salt for a few seconds to mix. Scatter the butter pieces over the flour mixture and pulse just until a ball of dough starts to form. Or, in a medium bowl, whisk the flour, 3 tablespoons sugar, and salt together. Cut in the butter pieces with a pastry cutter until the mixture forms large crumbs. ¶Briefly knead the dough by hand on a lightly floured surface to blend until smooth. Press the dough evenly into the bottom of the pan and bake in the center of the oven for about 15 to 17 minutes, or until light golden at the edges. ¶While the crust is baking, prepare the apricot topping. Drain the apricots and place in a food processor or a blender along with the remaining sugar. Pulse until the mixture is finely chopped, but not quite pureed. Add the egg, orange juice, and cream cheese. Process until creamy smooth. ¶Slowly pour the apricot mixture over the hot crust. Scatter the almonds over the filling. Immediately return the pan to the oven. Continue baking in the center of the oven for about 25 minutes, or until the filling is lightly browned around the edges. Let cool completely before cutting into 1- by 2-inch bars. Store in an airtight container.

Makes 32 bars

FIG OAT BARS

Dried Mission, Calimyrna, or Smyrna figs may be used to make these fruit-filled crumb bars. I find Mission figs plumpest, but prefer the flavor of Calimyrna and Smyrna figs. The milk, which produces a richer filling than water does, will look curdled while simmering.

8 ounces dried figs, stemmed and finely chopped

2 tablespoons granulated sugar

¾ cup milk or water

½ teaspoon ground nutmeg

1 tablespoon grated orange zest, or 1 teaspoon orange extract

1½ cups old-fashioned or quick (not instant) rolled oats

1½ cups all-purpose flour

1 cup firmly packed dark brown sugar

¼ teaspoon baking soda

½ teaspoon salt

½ teaspoon ground cinnamon

¾ cup (1½ sticks) unsalted butter, melted

¼ cup (1 ounce) walnuts, chopped

Preheat the oven to 350° F. Grease an 8-inch square baking pan. In a small saucepan over medium heat, simmer the figs, sugar, and milk or water for about 15 minutes, or until thickened. Stir in the nutmeg and orange zest or extract. Let cool a few minutes. ¶In a large bowl, with a large wooden spoon, combine the oats, flour, brown sugar, baking soda, salt, and cinnamon. Stir in the melted butter and walnuts. The mixture will be crumbly. Press about half of the dough firmly and evenly into the bottom of the pan. Spread the fig filling to within ¼ inch from the edge. Crumble the remaining oat mixture over the filling. ¶Bake in the center of the oven for about 25 to 30 minutes, or until lightly browned at the edges. Cool completely before cutting into bars. Store in an airtight container.

Makes 16 bars

Linzertorte Bars

Hazelnuts, cinnamon, lemon, and raspberry are the key flavors in this beautiful, lattice-topped Austrian pastry. I've researched many recipes and streamlined the preparation while keeping the Old World flavor. The small amount of cocoa tints the pastry a distinctive hue. These bars are worthy of a celebration.

1½ *cup all-purpose flour*
½ *cup (2 ounces) unskinned hazelnuts, ground*
1 *teaspoon Dutch process or plain unsweetened cocoa*
¼ *teaspoon baking powder*
¾ *teaspoon ground cinnamon*
⅛ *teaspoon ground cloves*
¼ *teaspoon salt*
½ *cup (1 stick) unsalted butter, softened*
⅔ *cup sugar*
1 *egg yolk*
1 *teaspoon grated lemon zest*
⅔ *cup raspberry jam, preferably with seeds*

Preheat the oven to 350° F. Grease an 8-inch square baking pan. In a medium bowl, whisk together the flour, hazelnuts, cocoa, baking powder, cinnamon, cloves, and salt; set aside. In a large bowl, with an electric mixer on low speed, cream the butter and sugar together. Mix in the egg yolk and lemon zest. Gradually blend in the flour mixture. Press 1 cup of the dough evenly into the bottom of the pan. Spread the raspberry jam to within ¼ inch of the edge. ¶On a lightly floured work surface, pat the remaining dough into a flat square. Place it between two sheets of waxed paper and use a rolling pin to roll the dough into an 8-inch square, about ¼ inch thick. Remove the top layer of the waxed paper. Use a pastry wheel or a blunt knife to cut the dough into sixteen ½-inch strips (a clear plastic ruler is a great help here). Spacing them evenly, place 8 strips across the raspberry jam layer. Place the remaining 8 strips perpendicular to the other strips, spacing them evenly to make a lattice. ¶Bake in the center of the oven for about 30 minutes, or until light brown around the edges. Let cool completely before cutting into bars. Store in an airtight container.

Makes 16 bars

HONEY GRANOLA BARS

Chewy, wholesome granola bars, loaded with oats, sunflower seeds, currants, almonds, and honey, are just the treat to take along on a hike. Wrap each bar individually to carry in a backpack.

1 cup all-purpose flour
1¾ cups old-fashioned or quick (not instant) rolled oats
1 teaspoon ground cinnamon
¼ teaspoon ground nutmeg
¼ teaspoon salt
½ cup firmly packed dark brown sugar
⅓ cup honey
⅔ cup (1⅓ sticks) unsalted butter, melted
¼ cup sunflower seeds
½ cup currants or raisins
½ cup sliced almonds

Preheat the oven to 350°F. Grease a 9-inch square baking pan. In a small bowl, whisk together the flour, oats, cinnamon, nutmeg, and salt; set aside. In a large bowl, with a wooden spoon, combine the brown sugar, honey, and melted butter. Blend in the flour mixture and stir in the sunflower seeds, currants or raisins, and almonds. ¶Press the dough firmly into the bottom of the pan. Bake in the center of the oven for about 30 minutes, or until light brown at the edges. Let cool completely before cutting into bars. Store in an airtight container. Well-wrapped bars may be frozen.

Makes 20 bars

CINNAMON SHORTBREAD

For large groups and fund-raisers, fragrant, appealing Cinnamon Shortbread is quick to make. Scottish in origin, shortbread derives its name from the fact that the dough is very "short," or rich in butter. A purist's cookie, it is traditionally made without eggs (handy to remember when you're out of eggs). Sometimes I make half a recipe and bake it in an 8-inch round cake pan to cut into wedges.

2 cups all-purpose flour
3½ teaspoons ground cinnamon
¼ teaspoon ground nutmeg
½ teaspoon salt
1 cup (2 sticks) unsalted butter, softened
½ cup sugar
¼ cup firmly packed light brown sugar
1 teaspoon pure vanilla extract

Preheat the oven to 350°F. Grease a 9- by 13-inch rectangular pan. In a small bowl, whisk the flour, cinnamon, nutmeg, and salt together; set aside. In a large bowl, with an electric mixer on low speed, cream the butter, sugar, and brown sugar together. Add the vanilla extract. Gradually blend the flour mixture into the butter mixture. Press the dough evenly into the bottom of the pan. Decoratively score the dough with a fork or small knife, if you wish. ¶Bake in the center of the oven for about 20 to 25 minutes, or until golden brown around the edges. Let cool completely before cutting into 2- by 2½-inch bars. Store in an airtight container. Well-wrapped shortbread may be frozen.

Makes 30 bars

CHERRY CHEESECAKE BARS

Layer a rich, cream cheese mixture, flavored with cherry jam, on a chocolate-almond crust to make luscious cheesecake in cookie form. To make cookie crumbs, place the cookies in a quart-sized plastic freezer bag, press out the air, and seal. Roll a heavy rolling pin back and forth to crush them to fine crumbs.

1 cup chocolate cookie crumbs (use homemade or purchased cookies)
¼ cup (1 ounce) almonds, ground
3 tablespoons sugar
5 tablespoons unsalted butter, melted

Cherry Cheesecake Topping
8 ounces cream cheese, softened and quartered
¼ cup sugar
1 large egg
¼ cup cherry jam
¼ teaspoon pure almond extract

Preheat the oven to 350° F. Grease an 8-inch square baking pan. In a medium bowl, combine the cookie crumbs, almonds, sugar, and melted butter. Press the crumbs evenly into the bottom of the pan. Use your fingers or the back of a spoon to smooth the surface. Bake in the center of the oven for 8 minutes. Transfer to a rack to cool while preparing the topping. ¶To make the topping: In a medium bowl, with an electric mixer on low speed, beat the cream cheese and sugar together. Mix in the egg, jam, and almond extract. Pour batter evenly over the crust, and level with a spatula. ¶Bake in the center of the oven for about 25 minutes, or until set but not browned. Let cool completely before cutting into bars. Store refrigerated in an airtight container.

Makes 16 bars

LEMON RASPBERRY BARS

For special occasions, serve these refreshing lemon raspberry bars. A delectable lemon cream cheese filling, strewn with fresh raspberries, is baked over a buttery shortbread crust. Blueberries are a lovely alternative, or the bars may be prepared without fruit.

1 cup (2 sticks) unsalted butter, softened
½ cup confectioners' sugar, sifted
2 cups all-purpose flour

Lemon Raspberry Filling
2 cups sugar
1 tablespoon all-purpose flour
3 ounces cream cheese, softened and halved
3 large eggs
⅓ cup fresh lemon juice
1 teaspoon pure lemon extract
Grated zest of 1 large lemon
2 tablespoons unsalted butter, melted and cooled
½ pint (1 cup) fresh raspberries or blueberries

Preheat the oven to 350° F. Grease a 9- by 13-inch baking pan. In a large bowl, with an electric mixer on low speed, cream the butter and confectioners' sugar together. Gradually beat in the flour. Continue to mix the dough just until it starts to form a ball. ¶Press the dough evenly in the bottom of the pan. Bake in the center of the oven for about 13 to 15 minutes, or until golden brown. Let cool for 10 minutes before topping with lemon raspberry filling. ¶To make the filling: In a large bowl, with an electric mixer on low speed, combine the sugar and flour together. Add the cream cheese and mix until smooth. Add the eggs, one at a time. Blend in the lemon juice, lemon extract, lemon zest, and melted butter. With a wooden spoon, gently stir in the raspberries. Carefully spoon the filling over the warm crust. Redistribute the raspberries in a random but fairly even pattern, if necessary. ¶Bake in the center of the oven for about 30 minutes, or until the edges are barely golden. Let cool briefly, then chill, covered, for 1 hour before cutting into bars. Store refrigerated in an airtight container.

Makes 24 bars

NEW ENGLAND BOILED CIDER BARS

Boiled cider, a thick, tart, amber syrup reduced from pure apple cider, gives a full-flavored apple taste to these custard and cookie crust bars. I have never made my own boiled cider, but if you wish to experiment boil 7 cups of cider until it reduces to 1 cup. Available by mail and from some stores in New England, boiled cider is a good, novel ingredient to have on hand. Refrigerate the unused portion.

½ cup (1 stick) unsalted butter, softened
3 tablespoons sugar
2 tablespoons firmly packed light brown sugar
¼ teaspoon ground nutmeg
⅛ teaspoon salt
1 cup all-purpose flour

Boiled Cider Custard

2 tablespoons all-purpose flour
½ cup real maple sugar or firmly packed light brown sugar and ¼
*   teaspoon pure maple flavoring*
¼ teaspoon each ground allspice, ground cloves, and ground cinnamon
½ cup heavy cream
2 large eggs
1 cup boiled cider

Preheat the oven to 350° F. Grease an 8-inch square baking pan. In a medium bowl, with an electric mixer on low speed, cream the butter, sugar, and brown sugar. Add the nutmeg and salt. Gradually add the flour. Mix the dough just until it is blended and smooth. Press the dough into the bottom of the pan. Bake in the center of the oven about 18 to 20 minutes, or until golden brown around the edges. Let cool for 10 minutes. ¶To make the custard: In a medium bowl, whisk together the flour, maple sugar or brown sugar and flavoring, allspice, cloves, and cinnamon. Whisk in the cream, then the eggs, and then the boiled cider. Using a large spoon, slowly ladle the custard over the warm crust (the crust can buckle if the filling is just poured on; this doesn't harm the flavor so don't be concerned if it happens). ¶Bake in the center of the oven for about 50 to 60 minutes, or until the custard appears firm (it will get firmer as it cools) and is lightly browned at the edges. Let cool completely before cutting into bars. Refrigerate in an airtight container.

Makes 16 bars

BROWNED BUTTER BARS

Browning the butter gives these simple-to-make bars a delicious butterscotch flavor. Add ¾ cup semisweet chocolate chips to the dough, if you like, to create a luxurious bar somewhat similar to a blondie.

1 cup all-purpose flour

½ teaspoon baking powder

½ teaspoon salt

6 tablespoons (¾ stick) unsalted butter

¾ cup firmly packed dark brown sugar

1 large egg

1½ teaspoons pure vanilla extract

½ cup (2 ounces) pecans, chopped

Preheat the oven to 350°F. Grease an 8-inch square baking pan. In a small bowl, whisk together the flour, baking powder, and salt; set aside. In a small, heavy saucepan over medium heat, melt the butter, stirring occasionally, until the butter browns but doesn't burn. Remove from the heat, and stir in the brown sugar. Mix in the egg and vanilla extract. Add the flour mixture to the butter mixture and stir until combined. Mix in the pecans. Spread the batter into the bottom of the pan. ¶Bake in the center of the oven for about 20 to 23 minutes, or until lightly browned at the edges. Let cool completely before cutting into bars. Store in an airtight container. Well-wrapped bars may be frozen.

Makes 16 bars

BUTTERY TOFFEE TRIANGLES

These bars look and taste as if they are difficult to make, but they aren't. They have the color and flavor of a toffee candy bar and are topped with a luscious layer of dark chocolate and almonds. This is a good spur-of-the-moment recipe and is especially nice to give as a gift.

1 cup all-purpose flour

¼ teaspoon salt

6 tablespoons (¾ stick) unsalted butter, softened

½ cup firmly packed light brown sugar

1 teaspoon pure vanilla extract

⅔ cup semisweet chocolate chips

⅓ cup (about 1½ ounces) slivered or sliced almonds

Preheat the oven to 350°F. Lightly grease an 8-inch square baking pan. In a small bowl, whisk the flour and salt together; set aside. In a medium bowl, with an electric mixer on low speed, cream the butter and brown sugar together. Mix in the vanilla extract. Gradually add the flour mixture, mixing until well combined. With a spatula, spread the dough evenly into the bottom of the pan. Bake in the center of the oven for about 20 to 25 minutes, or until golden brown. ¶Sprinkle the chocolate chips evenly over the hot crust. Cover the pan with a baking sheet for a minute or two to help retain heat to melt the chocolate. With the back of a spoon, spread the melted chocolate evenly to cover the surface. Sprinkle the almonds over the melted chocolate and press the nuts lightly to set. Let cool completely before cutting into bars. Store in an airtight container.

Makes 16 bars

BLACK WALNUT CHOCOLATE SQUARES

Pungent black walnuts, available by mail order, add a distinctive note to these bars. Regular English walnuts may also be used for a milder variation. For an attractive look, I slice the walnuts rather than chop them. Slice them ¼ inch wide, one nut at a time, on a cutting board using a small knife. A drizzle of chocolate makes for party fare.

½ cup (1 stick) unsalted butter, softened
¼ teaspoon salt
⅓ cup sugar
1 cup all-purpose flour
¾ cup (3 ounces) black or English walnuts, sliced or chopped
Chocolate Glaze (recipe follows)

Preheat the oven to 350°F. Grease an 8-inch square baking pan. In a medium bowl, with an electric mixer on medium speed, cream the butter, salt, and sugar together until pale in color. Stir in the flour and walnuts. ¶Press the dough evenly into the bottom of the pan. Bake in the center of the oven for about 23 to 25 minutes, or until lightly browned at the edges. Let cool. ¶Make the chocolate glaze. Use a small spoon to drizzle the glaze over the cookies in a random pattern. Let cool completely before cutting into bars. Store in an airtight container.

Makes 16 bars

Chocolate Glaze

1 tablespoon unsalted butter
1 square (1 ounce) semisweet or bittersweet chocolate, chopped

In a double boiler over barely simmering water, melt the butter and chocolate together, stirring until smooth. Set aside to cool slightly.

PECAN DIAMONDS

Pecans and caramel are a winning duo on a thin pastry crust. I prefer the look of whole pecans, but chopped pecans are fine. Other nuts may be substituted for wonderful variations on a theme. These rich bars are packed with flavor and should be cut into small diamonds or bars.

1¼ cups all-purpose flour
⅛ teaspoon ground cinnamon
¼ teaspoon salt
6 tablespoons (¾ stick) cold unsalted butter, cut into ¼-inch pieces
1 to 2 tablespoons ice water

Pecan Topping

6 tablespoons (¾ stick) unsalted butter
⅔ cup firmly packed light brown sugar
3 tablespoons mild honey
1 tablespoon half-and-half
2 teaspoons pure vanilla extract
2 cups (8 ounces) pecans, whole or chopped

In a food processor, combine the flour, cinnamon, and salt. Scatter the butter over the flour mixture. Pulse until the mixture forms large crumbs. Sprinkle 1 tablespoon of ice water over the mixture and pulse just until dough begins to form a ball. Add more water if necessary, 1 teaspoon at a time. Or, in a medium bowl, combine the flour, cinnamon, and salt. Cut in the butter with a pastry cutter until large crumbs form. Sprinkle 1 table-spoon of ice water over the flour mixture and mix until the dough can be gathered into a ball. Add more water if necessary, 1 teaspoon at a time. Wrap the dough well in plastic wrap and chill for 1 hour, or until firm. ¶Preheat the oven to 375°F. Grease an

8-inch square baking pan. On a lightly floured surface, with a floured rolling pin, roll the dough out ⅛ inch thick. Lift the dough occasionally to check if it is sticking, and lightly reflour the surface as needed. Fold the dough in half and place it in the pan with the fold at the center of the pan. Unfold the dough and press it into place on the bottom and slightly up the sides of the pan. Trim the pastry edge level all around. Bake in the center of the oven for about 12 minutes or until light golden brown. ¶To make the topping: In a medium, heavy saucepan, melt the butter over medium heat. Stir in the brown sugar and honey. Bring to a boil for 2 minutes. Remove from the heat and stir in the half-and-half and vanilla extract. Add the pecans, stirring to coat them evenly. Carefully spread the topping evenly over the warm crust. ¶Bake in the center of the oven for about 20 to 25 minutes, or until the topping just begins to brown. Let cool completely before cutting into bars. Store in an airtight container.

Makes 16 bars

BROWNIES

Perfect brownies should be moist, dense, and rich with chocolate. To accomplish this, mix the brownies by hand (to help prevent air being whipped in, therefore making them lighter in texture) and bake them just until set for fudgy results. It is difficult to test a brownie for doneness; it should pull away from the pan a little bit and a toothpick inserted in the center of the pan should come out with moist crumbs on it, not wet batter. But since all ovens bake differently, the *best* way is to note the amount of time the brownies were baked, critique the results, and adjust the time accordingly.

6 *tablespoons (¾ stick) unsalted butter*
3 *squares (3 ounces) unsweetened chocolate, chopped*
½ *cup all-purpose flour*
¼ *teaspoon salt*
⅛ *teaspoon ground cinnamon*
2 *large eggs*
1 *teaspoon instant coffee granules*
1 *cup plus 2 tablespoons sugar*
2 *teaspoons pure vanilla extract*

Preheat the oven to 350°F. Grease and flour an 8-inch square baking pan. In a double boiler over barely simmering water, melt the butter and chocolate together, stirring until smooth. Set aside to cool slightly. ¶In a small bowl, whisk together the flour, salt, and cinnamon; set aside. In a medium bowl, with a wooden spoon, beat the eggs, instant coffee granules, sugar, and vanilla extract together until well combined. Stir the melted chocolate into the sugar mixture, blending well. Fold in the flour mixture just until blended. ¶Pour the batter into the prepared pan, level the surface with a spatula, and place the pan on the center rack of the oven. Bake for about 23 to 28 minutes, or until set but not browned. Do not overbake. Let cool completely before cutting into 2-inch squares. Store in an airtight container. Well-wrapped brownies may be frozen.

Makes 16 bars

Variations

Chocolate Chunk Brownies: Stir 6 ounces of semisweet or bittersweet chocolate, cut into small chunks, or 1 cup of semisweet chocolate chips into the brownie batter and bake as directed in the main recipe.

Chocolate Glazed Brownies: In a small, heavy saucepan, melt 3 tablespoons of butter over medium heat. Remove from the heat and add ¾ cup semisweet chocolate chips, stirring until melted. Spread the warm glaze evenly over the cooled baked brownies. If you like, immediately sprinkle ½ cup (about 2 ounces) of chopped, slivered, or sliced nuts over the glaze. Let the glaze cool completely before cutting the brownies.

Brazil Nut Brownies: Stir 1 cup (about 5 ounces) of chopped Brazil nuts into the brownie batter or sprinkle over the surface of the unbaked brownies; bake as directed in the main recipe. Any nuts you like may be substituted.

White Chocolate Chunk Hazelnut Brownies: Stir 1 cup of vanilla milk chips or white chocolate chunks into the brownie batter and sprinkle ½ cup (2½ ounces) of chopped hazelnuts over the surface and bake as directed in the main recipe.

MARBLEIZED PEANUT BUTTER FUDGE BROWNIES

These eye-catching brownies are a hit at parties. The dramatic marbleized effect is surprisingly easy to achieve.

1 *cup all-purpose flour*
¼ *teaspoon baking powder*
½ *teaspoon salt*
¾ *cup (1½ sticks) unsalted butter*
3 *squares (3 ounces) unsweetened chocolate, finely chopped*
3 *large eggs*
1⅓ *cups firmly packed dark brown sugar*
1½ *teaspoons pure vanilla extract*

Peanut Butter Topping
¾ *cup creamy peanut butter*
¼ *cup sugar*
1 *tablespoon all-purpose flour*
¼ *teaspoon ground cinnamon*
6 *tablespoons half-and-half*

Preheat the oven to 350°F. Grease a 9- by 13-inch rectangular baking pan. In a small bowl, whisk together the flour, baking powder, and salt together; set aside. In the top of a double boiler over barely simmering water, melt the butter and chocolate, stirring until smooth. Set aside to cool slightly. ¶In a medium bowl, whisk together the eggs, brown sugar, and vanilla extract. Gradually stir in the melted chocolate mixture. Slowly stir the flour mixture into the chocolate batter. Pour the batter into the prepared pan. ¶To make the topping: In a medium bowl, with an electric mixer on low speed, combine the peanut butter, sugar, flour, cinnamon and cream together, mixing until well blended. Place in a small plastic bag and twist the top to close. Snip ½ inch off a bottom corner of the bag and squeeze about 6 lines of peanut butter batter (use all of it) across the fudge batter, parallel to the short side of the pan. Rotate the pan a half turn and, starting close to one side of the pan, pull a chopstick (or the narrow handle of a wooden spoon) through the dough, almost touching the bottom of the pan, perpendicular to the lines of peanut butter. Move the chopstick over about 1½ inches and pull the chopstick in the opposite direction to the other side of pan. Repeat this until the whole surface is marbleized. Voila! ¶Bake in the center of the oven for about 25 minutes, or until firm to a light touch. Let cool completely before cutting into bars. Store in an airtight container. Well-wrapped brownies may be frozen.

Makes 24 bars

White Chocolate Mint Brownies

The pale green mint stripe running through the middle of these dark chocolate brownies is a delicious surprise. The mint layer is made with melted white chocolate flavored with oil of peppermint or peppermint extract. The oil is expensive, but it is much more concentrated. These brownies take about an hour longer to prepare than regular brownies.

White Chocolate Mint Layer

4½ ounces white chocolate, chopped, or ¾ cup vanilla milk chips
5 or 6 drops oil of peppermint, or 1 teaspoon peppermint extract
Green food coloring (optional)

Brownie Batter

½ cup (1 stick) unsalted butter
4 squares (4 ounces) unsweetened chocolate, chopped
1¼ cups sugar
¼ teaspoon salt
2 large eggs
2 teaspoons pure vanilla extract
½ cup all-purpose flour

Neatly line the inside of an 8-inch square baking pan with aluminum foil and butter the bottom. In the top of a double boiler over barely simmering water, melt the white chocolate, stirring until smooth. Stir in the oil of peppermint or extract and optional drop of green food coloring. Using a rubber spatula, evenly spread the mint layer into the prepared pan. Cover and chill until firm. This may be done several hours ahead. ¶To make the brownie batter: Preheat the oven to 350°F. Grease an 8-inch square baking pan.

In the top of a double boiler set over barely simmering water, melt the butter and chocolate, stirring until smooth. Set aside to cool slightly. In a large bowl, with a wooden spoon, combine the sugar, salt, eggs, and vanilla. Add the chocolate mixture and mix well. Stir in the flour and mix the batter just until blended. Spread half of the batter into the bottom of the pan. ¶Remove the mint layer from the refrigerator. Carefully lift the foil out of the pan trying to keep the hardened mint layer intact, if possible. Breaks can be fixed, but the larger the piece the easier it is to use. Gently turn the mint layer over onto waxed paper and slowly pull off the foil. Use a pancake turner to lift the mint layer and place it on top of the brownie batter spread in the baking pan. Fit in any broken pieces. Spread the remaining batter over the mint layer, leveling the top. ¶Bake in the center of the oven for about 30 to 35 minutes, or until set but not browned. Let cool completely before cutting into bars. Store in an airtight container. Well-wrapped bars may be frozen.

Makes 16 bars

Milk Chocolate Coconut Brownies

In contrast to fudgy, moist brownies, these cakelike brownies have a light chocolate flavor somewhat like German chocolate cake, and a very rich chocolate-coconut topping. I have served these, uncut, as a birthday cake. If you wish to prepare your own fresh coconut, see page 25.

1 *cup all-purpose flour*
½ *cup sugar*
¼ *cup firmly packed light brown sugar*
½ *teaspoon baking soda*
½ *teaspoon salt*
½ *cup (1 stick) unsalted butter*
2 *tablespoons Dutch process or regular unsweetened cocoa*
½ *cup water*
1 *large egg*
¼ *cup plain yogurt*
1½ *teaspoons pure vanilla extract*
Chocolate Coconut Icing (recipe follows)

Preheat the oven to 375° F. Grease an 8-inch square baking pan. In a large bowl, whisk the flour, sugar, brown sugar, baking soda, and salt together; set aside. In a small saucepan, bring the butter, cocoa, and water to a boil over medium heat. Pour the hot chocolate mixture over the flour mixture and blend well. Mix the egg, yogurt, and vanilla extract together and add to the chocolate batter, blending well. Pour the batter into the prepared pan. ¶Bake in the center of the oven for about 25 to 30 minutes, or until the brownies spring back to a light touch. Prepare the icing and frost the warm brownies while still in the pan. Let the brownies cool before cutting into bars. Store in an airtight container.

Makes 16 bars

Chocolate Coconut Icing

4 *tablespoons (½ stick) unsalted butter*
¼ *cup half-and-half*
2 *tablespoons Dutch process or plain unsweetened cocoa*
1 *cup firmly packed light brown sugar*
¼ *teaspoon salt*
1½ *teaspoons pure vanilla extract*
⅔ *cup (2 ounces) shredded coconut*
½ *cup (2 ounces) pecans or walnuts, chopped*

In a medium saucepan over medium heat, bring the butter, half-and-half, and cocoa to a boil. Stir in the brown sugar and salt and cook until the sugar melts. Remove from the heat and mix in the vanilla extract, coconut, and pecans.

Raspberry Brownie Heart

A semisweet brownie, swirled with raspberry jam and baked in a heart-shaped pan, makes a good gift or special-occasion dessert.

½ *cup (1 stick) unsalted butter, softened*
3 *squares (3 ounces) unsweetened chocolate, chopped*
⅔ *cup all-purpose flour*
¼ *teaspoon baking powder*
¼ *teaspoon salt*
2 *large eggs*
¾ *cup firmly packed light brown sugar*
1½ *teaspoons pure vanilla extract*
½ *cup raspberry jam, preferably with seeds*

Preheat the oven to 350°F. Grease a heart-shaped baking pan with a maximum width and height of about 9 inches, or an 8-inch square baking pan. In the top of a double boiler over barely simmering water, melt the butter and chocolate together, stirring until smooth. Set aside to cool slightly. ¶In a small bowl, whisk the flour, baking powder, and salt together; set aside. In a medium bowl, beat together the eggs and brown sugar. Stir in the melted chocolate mixture and vanilla. Fold in the flour mixture just to combine. Pour the batter into the prepared pan. ¶Spoon about 4 lines of the raspberry jam, using all of it, across the pan on top of the dough (this doesn't have to be perfectly neat). Starting close to one side of the pan, pull a chopstick (or the narrow handle of a wooden spoon) through the dough, almost touching the bottom, perpendicular to the lines of raspberry jam. Move the chopstick over 1½ inches or so and pull the chopstick the other way. Keep moving the chopstick back and forth across the pan, spacing the lines about an inch apart (if the lines are too close together the surface will become muddled rather than marbled). ¶Bake in the center of the oven for about 25 to 30 minutes, or until set but not browned. Do not overbake. Let cool completely, then invert the pan and remove the brownie. Wrap in plastic wrap and store in an airtight container. Well-wrapped brownies may be frozen.

Makes 1 large heart or sixteen 2-inch squares

24-KARAT BROWNIES

Serve gilded brownies to herald festive times such as a silver or golden anniversary. The sharp contrast of the dark chocolate and brilliant 24-karat gold leaf (or silver leaf) is dramatically beautiful. People are fascinated to find that it has virtually no taste, and that it is edible and not harmful in small quantities. ¶The delicate process of applying the tissue-thin gold leaf with a gilder's tip (a flat, thin, long-haired brush about 3 inches wide) is intriguing. The materials needed are available by mail. Once, in the middle of learning the process, I breathed too close to the gold leaf, which caused it to fly away. Laughing did not help its retrieval. Gold and silver leaf is usually sold in "books" of squares, usually ranging in size from about 2 inches to 3½ inches. They are expensive, but only a little is used at a time. They have an indefinite shelf life, and the effect is spectacular.

1 batch Brownies (page 59), unmolded and uncut
4 to 6 squares of gold leaf*, depending on the gilder's tip

It is best to work in a draft-free room; gold leaf will fly easily. Hold the book of gold leaf close to the brownies. Slowly open the book and remove a leaf by touching it with the gilder's tip and pulling it away (in some books the gold leaf must be cut out, a tricky job) slide a protective piece of thin cardboard under the paper holding the gold leaf before cutting, to help prevent damage to other leaves. Slowly place the gold leaf on the upper left-hand quarter of the brownies and touch the leaf to the brownies. It should stick (if it hasn't already!). Lightly brush the surface of the leaf with the gilder's tip to make it adhere to the brownies. Repeat to cover the entire surface. ¶It is difficult to get a solid gold layer without patching, but the mottled effect is exquisite. Carefully cut the brownies into bars, if you wish, and store them in a single layer in an airtight container (a lot of handling may cause the gold to rub off). Well-wrapped ungilded brownies may be frozen.

Makes 16 gilded brownies
*All of the directions in the recipe apply equally to silver leaf.

ROLLED COOKIES

Children are big fans of rolled cookies. Flour may cover every square inch of the kitchen, but the glee is contagious as they roll out the dough and cut it into a potpourri of shapes. I have fond memories of a class of angelic three-year-olds who "oohed and aahed" as I tinted white icing into glorious colors with the tiniest bit of paste food coloring. They were spellbound as they decorated fat gingerbread cookies with that icing.

Of course, adults like the fun of making rolled cookies, as well. Some collect cookie cutters, especially antique ones, as a hobby. A few of my friends make their own. I have a basketful, but many times I design my own and cut templates out of posterboard to use as a guide. At the end of this book you will find several patterns and directions for making templates.

A heavy rolling pin, with or without handles, works extremely well to smoothly and evenly roll out the firm dough. Lightly dust it with flour before using. To prevent the dough from sticking, roll it out on a lightly floured surface or on a floured pastry cloth (which usually comes with a knitted pastry sleeve that slips over the rolling pin; use lightly floured). Both the rolling pin and the surface should be lightly refloured, as needed, to make sure the dough doesn't stick. Certain doughs may be rolled out between two sheets of waxed paper (this is noted in the recipes) for the quickest method. These doughs will be stiff. If necessary, add more of the liquid called for in the recipe, a teaspoon at a time.

Lightly roll the dough in different directions; lift up the dough and rotate it a quarter turn to make sure it isn't sticking to the surface. Some doughs are firmed by chilling to make them easier to roll out. If the recipe is large, dividing the dough in half before wrapping and chilling makes it easier to handle. It is important that the dough be rolled to an even thickness (usually 1/8 inch to 1/4 inch) so that the cut-out cookies will bake at the same rate (extra pressure on the edges will make them thinner). Check the thickness of the dough with a ruler, or place narrow slats of wood, the same thickness as you want the dough, on either side of the dough so that the rolling pin will eventually touch them (mine were custom-made). You may also buy rolling pin thickness guides that slip onto the pin itself, available by mail.

To cut out rolled cookies, begin close to one edge of the dough and press the cookie cutter into the dough. Zig-zag the rows of cut-out cookies as closely together as possible. If the cutter sticks to the dough, lightly flour it. Sometimes the cutter will hold the cut-out cookie in place; if so, just transfer it directly to a baking sheet. Otherwise, transfer the cut-out cookies to the baking sheet using a pancake turner. Reroll the scraps once or twice; they will toughen a bit because more flour is used each time. I bake the skeleton of scraps from the final roll-out as is (cut to fit on the baking sheet). It gets eaten or crushed into crumbs for pie crusts and fruit crisp toppings.

To clean the rolling pin, first scrape off any bits of dough with a hard rubber spatula or a plastic dough scraper, then hand wash. A rolling pin with handles shouldn't be washed directly under running water because it may rust the internal ball bearings. A dough scraper is also good to clean off a pastry board before washing.

CHOCOLATE SUGAR COOKIES

Sugar cookies are the classic rolled cookies, but *chocolate* sugar cookies are also great sandwiched with your favorite filling (try the Ganache on page 40), served plain, or decorated to your heart's content. The Dutch cocoa used here produces a mellow chocolate flavor.

2¼ *cups all-purpose flour*
¾ *cup unsweetened Dutch process cocoa*
½ *teaspoon salt*
1 *cup (2 sticks) unsalted butter, softened*
1⅞ *cups (2 cups less 2 tablespoons) confectioners' sugar, sifted*
1 *large egg*
2 *to 3 tablespoons heavy cream*
2 *teaspoons pure vanilla extract*

In a large bowl, whisk together the flour, cocoa, and salt; set aside. In a large bowl, with an electric mixer on medium speed, cream the butter and confectioners' sugar until pale in color. Mix in the egg, 2 tablespoons of the cream, and vanilla extract. On low speed, add the cocoa mixture gradually. The dough will be stiff. If the mixer balks, add more cream, 1 teaspoon at a time. Divide the dough in half and shape each half into a flattened ball. Wrap well with plastic wrap and chill for 15 minutes. ¶Preheat the oven to 350°F. On a lightly floured surface, use a lightly floured rolling pin to roll one half of the dough to a ³/₁₆-inch thickness. Lift the dough occasionally to check if it is sticking. Lightly reflour the work surface and rolling pin as needed. Cut out shapes with 2-inch cookie cutters and place them 1 inch apart on ungreased baking sheets. Reroll the scraps and cut out cookies. Repeat with the second dough half. ¶Bake in the center of the oven for about

9 to 11 minutes, or until set. Let the cookies cool on the baking sheet for a few minutes, then transfer them to a wire rack to cool completely. Store in an airtight container. Well-wrapped cookies may be frozen.

Makes about 4 dozen cookies

PENUCHE ALMOND COOKIES

Penuche (pronounced "pee-NOO-chee") is a seductive, creamy, brown sugar fudge with a Mexican accent that sparked the idea for these fancy, delectable almond cookies with a stripe of penuche icing.

2½ *cups all-purpose flour*
½ *teaspoon baking soda*
½ *teaspoon salt*
1 *cup (2 sticks) unsalted butter, softened*
1 *cup firmly packed light brown sugar*
1 *large egg*
1 *teaspoon pure vanilla extract*
½ *teaspoon pure almond extract*
About 4 *dozen blanched almond halves, slivers, or slices for decoration*
Penuche Icing *(recipe follows)*

In a medium bowl, whisk together the flour, baking soda, and salt; set aside. In a large bowl, with an electric mixer on medium speed, cream the butter and brown sugar together. Add the egg, vanilla extract, and almond extract. On low speed, gradually stir in the flour mixture and mix until well combined. Divide the

dough in half and shape each half into a flattened ball. Wrap tightly in plastic wrap and chill for 30 minutes. ¶Preheat the oven to 375°F. On a lightly floured surface, using a lightly floured rolling pin, roll half of the dough to a 3/16-inch thickness. Lift the dough occasionally to check if it is sticking. Lightly reflour the work surface and rolling pin as needed. Cut out cookies with a 2-inch cookie cutter. Place the cookies 1 inch apart on ungreased baking sheets. Press an almond half, flat side down, in the center of each cookie. Reroll the scraps and cut out cookies. Repeat with the second half of dough. ¶Bake in the center of the oven for about 8 to 10 minutes, or until set but not browned. Let the cookies cool on the baking sheet for a few minutes, then transfer them to a wire rack to cool completely. ¶Slowly drizzle a wide stripe of warm icing across each cookie, over the almond. Let the icing dry completely before storing the cookies in an airtight container. Well-wrapped cookies may be frozen.

Makes about 4 dozen cookies

Penuche Icing

4 *tablespoons (½ stick) unsalted butter*
½ *cup firmly packed light brown sugar*
2 *tablespoons heavy cream*
⅔ *cup confectioners' sugar, sifted*
¼ *teaspoon pure vanilla extract*
⅛ *teaspoon salt*

In a small saucepan over medium heat, melt the butter with the brown sugar and cream; boil for 1 minute. Stir in the confectioners' sugar, vanilla extract, and salt; mix until smooth. Transfer to a small pitcher or measuring cup and use warm.

DEVON CREAM SUGAR COOKIES

The region of Devon, England, is famous for the thick, luscious double cream that inspired these iced sugar cookies. Outside of Britain, Devon cream can be found in gourmet and specialty foods stores, but it isn't essential because regular heavy cream also works very well.

3 *cups all-purpose flour*
1½ *teaspoons baking powder*
½ *teaspoon salt*
1 *cup (2 sticks) unsalted butter, softened*
1 *cup sugar*
1 *large egg*
¼ *cup Devon double cream or heavy cream*
1¼ *teaspoons pure vanilla extract*
Vanilla Glaze (recipe follows)

Preheat the oven to 350°F. Lightly grease the baking sheets. In a medium bowl, whisk together the flour, baking powder, and salt; set aside. In a large bowl, with an electric mixer on medium speed, cream the butter and sugar together until pale in color. Mix in the egg. On low speed, add about half of the flour mixture. Add the cream and vanilla extract. Slowly add the remaining flour and mix the dough until thoroughly blended. ¶Divide the dough in half and shape each half into a flattened ball. Wrap the dough tightly in plastic wrap and chill for 30 minutes or until firm enough to handle. It may be chilled overnight. ¶On a lightly floured surface, using a lightly floured rolling pin, roll half of the dough ¼ inch thick. Lift the dough occasionally to check if it is sticking. Lightly reflour the work surface and rolling pin as needed. Cut out the cookies with a 2½-inch cutter and place them 1 inch apart on the baking sheets.

Reroll the scraps and cut out cookies. Repeat with the second half of dough. ¶Bake in the center of the oven for about 10 to 12 minutes, or until just set but not brown around the edges. Let the cookies cool on the baking sheet for a few minutes, then transfer them to a wire rack to cool completely. ¶Prepare the vanilla glaze: Use a pastry brush or small spatula to frost the cookies while they are still warm (this causes a nice sheen). Let the cookies dry thoroughly. Store in an airtight container between sheets of waxed paper to prevent icing smudges. Well-wrapped cookies may be frozen.

Makes about 3 dozen cookies

Vanilla Glaze
1¾ *cups confectioners' sugar, sifted*
¼ *cup Devon double cream or heavy cream*
2 *teaspoons pure vanilla extract*
¼ *teaspoon salt*

In a small bowl, whisk together all ingredients until smooth.

PASTELS

These delicate cookies sandwiched with four flavors of pastel fillings have a retro look to them, as if they belonged at a fifties tea party. They are delightful for company because of the novelty of their flavors: The pink filling is flavored with rose essence; the purple filling is flavored with violet essence; the yellow filling is flavored with Grand Marnier; and the white filling is flavored with almond extract. Rose essence can be found in East Indian food stores; I found the violet essence in London. If you prefer, fruit flavors such as orange extract, lemon extract, lime extract, and black currant flavoring may be substituted, but there are many novel flavors available by mail.

2 *cups all-purpose flour*
3 *tablespoons sugar*
¼ *teaspoon salt*
¾ *cup (1½ sticks) cold butter, cut into ¼-inch pieces*
2 *to 3 tablespoons half-and-half*
Pastel Filling (recipe follows)

In a food processor, combine the flour, sugar, and salt. Scatter the butter over the flour and process until the mixture forms large crumbs. Sprinkle 2 tablespoons of the half-and-half over the flour mixture and process briefly, just until the mixture starts to come together. If necessary, add the remaining half-and-half 1 teaspoon at a time and process briefly. Or, in a medium bowl, whisk together the flour, sugar, and salt. Cut in the butter with a pastry cutter. Sprinkle 2 tablespoons of the half-and-half over all and stir until mixture comes together to form a ball. If needed, add the remaining half-and-half 1 teaspoon at a time. Briefly knead the dough by hand to gather in loose crumbs. Divide the dough in half and shape each half into a flattened ball. Tightly cover with plastic wrap and chill for 30 minutes or overnight. ¶Preheat the oven to 350°F. On a lightly floured surface, using a lightly floured rolling pin, roll out one half of the dough ⅛-inch thick. Lift the dough occasionally to check if it is sticking. Lightly reflour the work surface and rolling pin as needed. Cut out cookies using a 1½-inch cutter. Reroll the scraps and cut out cookies until all the dough is used. Repeat with the second half of dough. Place 1 inch apart on ungreased baking sheets. Bake for about 9 to 11 minutes, or until firm but not browned. Let the cookies cool on the baking sheet for a few minutes, then transfer them to a wire rack to cool completely. ¶Make the pastel filling. Divide the cookies into four groups. Assemble the cookies one group at a time: Spread a ⅛-inch layer of rose filling on the bottom side of a cookie and place another cookie, bottom side touching the filling, on top. Press together to make a sandwich. Repeat with the remaining cookies in that group. Repeat with the remaining three fillings and three groups of cookies. Store in an airtight container. The cookies will soften on standing.

Makes about 4 dozen sandwich cookies

Pastel Filling

⅔ cup (1⅓ sticks) unsalted butter, softened
2½ cups confectioners' sugar, sifted
2 to 3 tablespoons half-and-half
¼ teaspoon salt
Red, yellow, and violet food coloring (liquid or paste)
About ¼ teaspoon each rose essence, violet essence, almond extract, and Grand Marnier

In a medium bowl, combine the butter, confectioners' sugar, 2 tablespoons half-and-half, and salt and beat until fluffy and spreadable. Add more half-and-half, 1 teaspoon at a time, if necessary to achieve a spreadable consistency. ¶Divide the filling equally among 4 small bowls. Using a tiny amount of food coloring (especially if using paste) tint 1 portion pale pink, 1 portion pale yellow, and 1 portion pale purple. Leave the remaining portion white. Add ¼ teaspoon of flavoring, or to taste, to each bowl as follows: rose essence to the pink, Grand Marnier to the yellow, violet essence to the purple, and almond extract to the white.

CACTUS COOKIES

These simple, decorated sugar cookies are an entertaining finale to a Mexican meal. The cookie dough may be tinted pale green, if you wish, and decorated with a slightly darker green icing. The finished cookies should be arranged in a single layer, because the butter cream icing may smudge. Royal icing flowers to decorate some of the cactus are inexpensive and useful to have on hand. Baking supply stores and mail order resources carry them (see page 118). Or you may handmake them with a pastry bag fitted with a special tip, see page 25.

3¾ cups all-purpose flour
½ teaspoon baking powder
½ teaspoon salt
1⅓ cups (2⅔ sticks) unsalted butter, softened
1 cup sugar
1 large egg
1½ teaspoons pure vanilla extract
Green Butter Cream Icing (recipe follows)
Royal icing flowers (about 1 per cookie)

In a medium bowl, whisk together the flour, baking powder, and salt; set aside. In a large bowl, with an electric mixer on medium speed, cream the butter and sugar together until fluffy. Stir in the egg and vanilla extract. On low speed, slowly add the flour, combining well. Divide the dough in half and shape each into a flattened ball. Cover with plastic wrap and chill for 1 hour or overnight. ¶Preheat the oven to 375°F. On a lightly floured surface using a lightly floured rolling pin, roll out half of the dough ¼ inch thick. Lift the dough occasionally to check if it is sticking. Lightly reflour the work surface and rolling pin as needed. Cut out the cactus shapes with a cutter and place cookies

2 inches apart on ungreased baking sheets. Reroll the scraps and cut out cookies. Repeat with the second half of dough. ¶Bake in the center of the oven for about 10 to 12 minutes, or until just starting to turn golden at the edges. Let the cookies cool on baking sheets for a few minutes, then transfer them to a wire rack to cool completely before decorating. ¶To decorate frost the cookies with the darker green icing, using a small spatula; fit a pastry bag with a plain No. 3 tip or a small leaf tip and fill halfway with pale green icing. Twist the top of the bag closed. Hold the bag at a 45-degree angle and squeeze gently to outline or decorate a cookie. Immediately press a royal icing flower into the fresh icing. Let the cookies dry completely. Store in an airtight container. Well-wrapped unfrosted cookies may be frozen.

Makes about 2 dozen cookies

Green Butter Cream Icing

1 box (1 pound) confectioners' sugar (about 3½ to 4 cups), sifted
1 cup (2 sticks) unsalted butter, softened
¼ teaspoon salt
1 teaspoon pure vanilla extract
2 tablespoons milk
Green food coloring (paste or liquid)

In a large bowl, with an electric mixer on low speed, beat the confectioners' sugar, butter, salt, vanilla extract, and milk together until smooth. Use a bit of food coloring to tint ¾ of the icing to the shade of green desired (or make several different shades for a pleasant effect). Tint the remaining icing palest green to use to pipe details.

MAPLE SUGAR LEAVES

Real maple sugar (available by mail) is easy to bake with. It delivers pure, natural maple flavor without the stickiness of maple syrup. Light brown sugar can be substituted with good (but different) flavor results, but do not substitute maple syrup. ¶Bake the cookies in three large, simplified leaf shapes: sugar maple, oak, and birch. Find beautiful leaves, and make posterboard templates following the directions on page 115. Maple icing, tinted in the brilliantly colored hues of autumn, may be painted onto the cookies with a pastry brush.

2 cups all-purpose flour
1 teaspoon baking powder
½ teaspoon salt
⅛ teaspoon ground nutmeg
¾ cup (1½ sticks) unsalted butter, softened
¾ cup plus 2 tablespoons pure maple sugar (not maple syrup) or light brown sugar and ½ teaspoon pure maple flavoring (not imitation)
1 large egg
Maple Icing (recipe follows)

In a medium bowl, whisk together the flour, baking powder, salt, and nutmeg; set aside. In a large bowl, with an electric mixer on medium speed, cream the butter and maple sugar or brown sugar and flavoring together. Add the egg. On low speed, gradually stir the flour mixture into the butter mixture and mix well. Divide the dough in half and shape each half into a flattened ball. Wrap well in plastic wrap and chill for 30 minutes or overnight. ¶Preheat the oven to 350°F. On a lightly floured surface using a lightly floured rolling pin, roll out one half of the dough at a time, ¼ inch thick. Lift the dough occasionally to check if it is sticking. Lightly reflour the work surface and rolling pin as needed. Cut

out the cookies with leaf-shaped cutters or by drawing around templates with a small, sharp paring knife or an X-acto knife (if using the template method, roll the dough out on a large cutting board). Place the cookies 2 inches apart on ungreased baking sheets. Reroll the scraps and cut out cookies. Repeat with the second half of dough. Bake in the center of the oven for about 10 to 12 minutes, or until set. Let cool on the baking sheet for a few minutes, then transfer to a wire rack to cool completely. Prepare the Maple Icing. ¶Use a 1-inch pastry brush to freely glaze the cookies with maple icing in the colors you like. Let several colors run together to create a beautiful effect. (You may want to look at photographs of fall foliage for inspiration.) Clean the brush, as needed, to prevent the colors from turning muddy. Let the cookies dry completely. Store in an airtight container. Well-wrapped unfrosted cookies may be frozen.

Makes about 1 dozen assorted large leaves

Maple Icing
2 cups confectioners' sugar, sifted
3 tablespoons water
¼ teaspoon salt
½ teaspoon pure maple flavoring (not imitation)
Red, orange, brown, golden yellow, and leaf green
*   paste food coloring*

In a medium bowl, whisk together the confectioners' sugar, water, salt, and maple flavoring until blended. The icing should be just thin enough to glaze a cookie using a pastry brush, but thick enough to be fairly opaque. ¶Divide the icing into 5 small bowls. Use a toothpick to transfer a different dot of paste food coloring to each bowl, then mix well to blend the color. Use a clean toothpick for each transfer. Cover the icing with plastic wrap touching the surface of the icing to prevent a crust from forming.

BABY CAKES

Children like to help make (and eat) these colorful, miniature cookies in fun shapes. Tiny cookie cutters, purchased as a set in a toy store, are suitable for small hands to use. The baked cookies can be painted with colorful icing. This cookie dough has nutritious, easy-to-digest arrowroot in it and rolls out easily between sheets of waxed paper—there's no messy flouring involved. Arrowroot is available in the spice section of most supermarkets.

7 tablespoons (⅞ stick) unsalted butter, softened
⅓ cup firmly packed light brown sugar
½ teaspoon pure vanilla extract
¼ teaspoon pure orange extract, or 2 drops pure orange oil
1 cup all-purpose flour
2 tablespoons arrowroot
⅛ teaspoon salt
Icing (recipe follows)

Preheat the oven to 350° F. Grease the baking sheets. In a medium bowl, with an electric mixer on low speed, cream the butter and brown sugar together. Mix in the vanilla extract and orange extract or oil. In a small bowl, whisk the flour, arrowroot, and salt until blended; add to the butter mixture and mix well. ¶Roll the dough out ¼ inch thick between 2 sheets of waxed paper. Remove the top sheet of waxed paper and cut out the shapes with assorted 1¼-inch cookie cutters. Place the cookies ½ inch apart on the baking sheets. Bake in the center of the oven for about 7 to 8 minutes, or until set but not browned. Let cool on baking sheets for a few minutes, then transfer to a cool surface to cool completely (very small cookies fall through most wire racks).

Prepare the icing. ¶Use a pastry brush or clean watercolor brush to paint the cookies. Let dry. Store in an airtight container. Well-wrapped unfrosted cookies may be frozen.

Makes about 5 dozen cookies

Icing

2 cups confectioners' sugar, sifted
3 tablespoons milk
Red, yellow, purple, and turquoise food coloring

In a small bowl, whisk the confectioners' sugar and milk until smooth. Divide the icing into 4 cups and tint with food coloring. Cover the icing with plastic wrap touching the surface of the icing to prevent a crust from forming.

Gingerbread Bears

Gingerbread has been an international favorite for hundreds of years. Research suggests that the ancient Chinese and Greeks had honey ginger cakes around 2800 B.C. In the Middle Ages, decorative forms of gingerbread were found all over Europe. England had popular gingerbread stalls at medieval fairs, and Germany was noted for its gingerbread houses. ¶The fragrance and flavor of spices combined with molasses are hard to resist. Trace or draw your favorite bear from an old photograph or illustration and make a template (page 115). Sometimes I blow up the design on a copy machine, to about 12 inches. The huge bear cookie makes a good gift, especially with a ribbon tied around the neck. Any cookie cutters or design you wish may be used here.

½ teaspoon each salt and baking soda
2 teaspoons ground ginger
2 teaspoons ground cinnamon
½ teaspoon ground cloves
½ teaspoon ground cardamom (optional)
3¼ cups all-purpose flour
¾ cup (1½ sticks) unsalted butter, softened
¾ cup sugar
¾ cup unsulfured molasses
¼ cup water
Royal Icing (recipe follows)

In a medium bowl, whisk the salt, baking soda, ginger, cinnamon, cloves, cardamom, and flour; set aside. In a large bowl, with an electric mixer on medium speed, cream the butter and sugar together until fluffy. Stir in the molasses and water; the mixture will look curdled. On low speed, gradually add the flour mixture to butter mixture, mixing well. Divide the dough in half and shape each half into a flattened ball. Wrap in plastic wrap and chill for 1 hour or overnight. The dough may by frozen at this point, but it must be thawed completely before using. ¶Preheat the oven to 350°F. Lightly grease the baking sheets. On a lightly floured surface, with a lightly floured rolling pin, roll out one half of the dough ¼ inch thick. Lift the dough occasionally to check if it is sticking. Lightly reflour the work surface and rolling pin as needed. ¶Cut out the cookies by tracing around the bear template with the tip of a small, sharp knife (or X-acto knife), mark key details such as eyes, and transfer the cookies to the baking sheets, using 2 spatulas or pancake turners, if needed. When making very large cookies, the dough can also be rolled and cut out directly on the baking sheets (place a dish towel underneath the baking sheet to help keep it from moving) to avoid the distortion caused by being moved. Repeat with the second half of dough. Reroll scraps and cut out cookies. ¶Bake in the center of the oven for about 13 to 15 minutes, or until set. Let the cookies cool on baking sheets for a few minutes, then transfer them to a wire rack to cool completely before decorating. ¶Make the royal icing. Fit a pastry bag with a No. 3 or No. 4 round tip and fill the bag half full with icing; firmly twist the top of the bag closed. Hold the bag at a 45-degree angle and squeeze gently to outline and decorate the cookie. Let dry for 24 hours. Store in an airtight container. Well-wrapped, undecorated cookies may be frozen.

Royal Icing

1 *cup confectioners' sugar, sifted*
1 *large egg white (or meringue powder, according to manufacturer's instructions)*
Scant ¼ teaspoon cream of tartar
¼ teaspoon pure orange or lemon extract

In a large bowl, with an electric mixer on low speed, combine the confectioners' sugar, egg white or meringue powder, cream of tartar, and orange or lemon extract. Beat on medium-high speed for about 5 minutes, or until peaks of icing can be formed with a spoon. If peaks can't be formed after 5 minutes, beat icing at a higher speed for a minute or two. Take care; if the icing is overbeaten it may break down. It is best to use the icing right away; keep it tightly covered when not in use. Tint icing if you wish.

Makes five 8-inch bears

A ROSE-SCENTED CUPID AND VALENTINE HEARTS

Hearts, flowers, and cupids are the quintessential symbols of Valentine's Day, and this cookie combines all three elements. The crystallized rosebuds, pistachio nuts, and silver and pink dragées are held in place with tinted royal icing. Rose essence delicately scents the cookie; the flavor is unexpected and pleasant. I've found rose essence (also called extract) in London's Fortnum & Mason and in East Indian markets in the United States and Europe. You also may find it in specialty foods stores, or order it by mail, see page 116. To make a cupid template trace or draw your favorite illusration and enlarge to 8 inches. See page 115. ¶This cupid could also be a Christmas or New Year's angel.

¾ *cup (1½ sticks) unsalted butter, softened*
¾ *cup confectioners' sugar, sifted*
¼ *teaspoon salt*
2 *cups all-purpose flour*
¼ *teaspoon rose essence or pure almond extract*
1 *tablespoon milk*
Red food coloring (paste or liquid)
Royal Icing (recipe above), made without orange or lemon extract
14 *crystallized rosebuds*
28 *pistachio slivers*
Pink and silver dragées

In a medium bowl, with an electric mixer on medium speed, cream the butter, confectioners' sugar, and salt together until pale in color. On low speed, add the flour gradually. Mix in the rose essence or almond extract, and milk. Tint the dough pale pink with liquid red food coloring a drop at a time or 1 dot of red paste food coloring (using a clean toothpick). Blend the dough well to make the color uniform. Shape the dough into a ball, flatten it a bit and wrap well in plastic wrap. Chill the dough about 30 minutes or overnight. ¶Preheat the oven to 350°F. Lightly grease the baking sheets. With a rolling pin, roll the dough out between 2 sheets of waxed paper ¼ inch thick. Remove the top sheet of the waxed paper and flip the dough over directly onto the center of the baking sheet. Remove the waxed paper. Place the lightly floured template on the center of the dough. With a small, sharp knife or X-acto knife, cut all around as close to the template as possible. Remove the excess dough carefully and keep the scraps covered with plastic wrap. ¶Bake the cupid cookie on the center rack of the oven for about 15 to 18 minutes, or until firmly set but not browned at the edges. Let the cookie cool completely on the baking sheet, then very carefully loosen the cookie from baking sheet on all sides with a large spatula. Hold the baking sheet at the same level as the wire rack and use the spatula to slowly slide the cookie onto it to cool completely. ¶Reroll the scraps between 2 sheets of waxed paper. Remove the top sheet. Cut out the hearts with a 2-inch cookie cutter. Repeat with the remaining scraps. Place cookies 1 inch apart on a lightly greased baking sheet. Bake in the center of the oven for about 9 to 13 minutes, or until set but not browned. Let the cookies cool on the baking sheet for a few minutes, then transfer them to a wire rack to cool completely. ¶Make the royal icing. Tint the icing with food coloring to match the cookies. Use a toothpick to coat the back of the decorations with a bit of icing. Place 2 rosebuds on the cupid cookie at the top of the heart. Place 2 pistachio slivers under each rosebud to form the leaves. Place the silver dragées to form stems under the leaves and on the tips of the wings. Place the pink dragées on the toes. Echo this flower motif on the heart cookies using 1 rosebud per cookie. You may find it easier to dot a little icing directly on the cookie, then place the decoration on top. Let the cookies dry overnight, preferably 24 hours. Store in an airtight container. Well-wrapped undecorated cookies may be frozen.

Makes 1 cupid and 1 dozen 2-inch hearts

GRAHAM CRACKERS

The very idea of homemade graham crackers is appealing. Graham flour is the coarsely ground whole-wheat flour named after Sylvester Graham, a proponent of whole wheat. If you can't find graham flour, use regular whole-wheat flour. The dough is rolled out and marked directly on the baking sheet. The delicious, thin cookies will break apart with a satisfying snap.

¾ cup all-purpose flour
½ cup graham or whole-wheat flour
½ teaspoon ground cinnamon
¼ teaspoon baking soda
¼ teaspoon salt
4 tablespoons (½ stick) unsalted butter, softened
⅓ cup firmly packed dark brown sugar
¼ cup unsulfured molasses
1 teaspoon pure vanilla extract
1 to 3 teaspoons water (optional)

Preheat the oven to 350°F. Grease a 15½- by 12-inch or larger baking sheet, or use two smaller pans and bake half of the dough at a time . ¶In a medium bowl, whisk together the flour, graham or whole-wheat flour, cinnamon, baking soda, and salt; set aside. In a large bowl, with an electric mixer on low speed, cream the butter and sugar together. Add the molasses and vanilla extract. Gradually add the flour mixture to the molasses mixture and mix until well blended. The dough will be stiff. If necessary, add water 1 teaspoon at a time to soften the dough. ¶With a floured rolling pin, roll the dough out directly on the baking sheet (a dish towel underneath the baking sheet will keep it from slipping) to an ⅛-inch thickness, forming a rough 10-inch by 12-inch rectangle. The edges will be uneven. Graham crackers should be crisp, so make sure the dough is rolled thin. ¶Using a ruler if you wish (a clear plastic one works well), cut 1-inch vertical strips with a blunt knife or smooth-edged pastry wheel. Cut 3-inch horizontal strips and prick each rectangle with a fork. Bake the graham crackers, with the scraps at the sides intact, on the center rack of the oven for about 13 to 15 minutes, or until lightly browned. Do not underbake. Let cool completely on the baking sheet. Break apart and store in an airtight container. Well-wrapped cookies may be frozen.

Makes 40 crackers

Variation

Baby Grahams: Use miniature cookie cutters in animal shapes for children's cookies.

GALETTES

These handsome, tasty cookies were inspired by French lemon-almond cakes. *Galette* is a French word that refers to several regional variations of cake and pastry. I associate the flavor of lemon with *galettes*, but they may contain all manner of flavorings. These have a decorative surface made by glazing and scoring the cookies *before* baking.

½ cup (1 stick) unsalted butter, softened
½ cup (5 ounces) almond paste, cut into chunks
3 tablespoons sugar
¾ teaspoon pure lemon extract
¼ teaspoon pure almond extract
1 cup all-purpose flour
¼ teaspoon salt

Glaze
1 large egg yolk
2 teaspoons water
¼ teaspoon pure almond extract

Preheat the oven to 375°F. Line the baking sheets with baking parchment or aluminum foil. In a medium bowl, with an electric mixer on low speed, beat the butter, almond paste, and sugar together until creamy. Add the lemon extract and almond extract. In a small bowl, whisk the flour and salt together and stir into the butter mixture. Knead the dough on waxed paper to blend it until smooth. With a rolling pin, roll the dough out ¼ inch thick between 2 sheets of waxed paper. Cut out the cookies with a 2-inch round cutter. Place 1½ inches apart on the baking

sheets. Reroll scraps and cut out cookies. ¶To make the glaze: Whisk all the ingredients in a small bowl. With a pastry brush, brush the glaze onto the cookies. Use a fork to score a design ⅛ inch deep on top of each cookie (a small canapé cutter also works well to mark a design when pressed ⅛ inch into the top of each cookie). ¶Bake in the center of the oven for about 8 to 10 minutes, or until golden brown (so that the design shows). Let the cookies cool on the baking sheet for a few minutes, then transfer them to a wire rack to cool completely. Store in an airtight container. Well-wrapped cookies may be frozen.

Makes about 1½ dozen cookies

Black Raspberry Rugelach

Rugelach, a distinctive rolled-up pastry, is popular in New York City, especially for breakfast. Some recipes have yeast or sour cream in them; this one has cream cheese in the dough. A black raspberry jam filling, enhanced with finely chopped nuts, raisins, and cinnamon sugar, is spread over the rolled-out circle of dough. It is then cut into wedges, then each wedge is rolled up into a pastry and baked.

½ cup (1 stick) unsalted butter, softened
3 ounces cream cheese, softened
¼ teaspoon pure lemon extract, or ¼ teaspoon grated lemon zest
¼ teaspoon ground cinnamon
¼ teaspoon salt
1 cup all-purpose flour

Black Raspberry Filling

½ cup black raspberry jam or your favorite thick jam
⅓ cup sugar
1¼ teaspoons ground cinnamon
⅓ cup currants or chopped raisins
½ cup (2 ounces) walnuts, finely chopped

In a medium bowl, with an electric mixer on low speed, cream the butter, cream cheese, lemon extract or zest, cinnamon, and salt together. Add the flour gradually. Knead by hand for a moment to gather in loose crumbs. Shape into a flattened ball. Cover with plastic wrap and chill for 1 hour or overnight. ¶Preheat the oven to 375° F. Grease a baking sheet or line it with baking parchment. On a lightly floured board, use a lightly floured rolling pin to roll the dough out to form a 13-inch round. The edges don't have to be perfectly even. ¶To make the filling: In a medium bowl, mix together all of the filling ingredients. Spread the filling evenly over the dough almost to the edge. Cut the dough into 16 equal wedges using a pastry wheel or table knife. Starting at the wide end, roll up each triangle and place it, point side down on the baking sheet, spacing the triangles 2 inches apart. ¶Bake in the center of the oven for about 15 to 20 minutes, or until golden. Let the pastries cool on the baking sheet for a few minutes, then transfer them to a wire rack to cool completely. Store in an airtight container. Well-wrapped rugelach may be frozen.

Makes 16 pastries

INDIAN PEACH PINWHEELS

I had never heard of Indian peaches until recently, when my Texan cousins gave me a home-canned jar of delicious preserves made from this variety of peach. They grow wild near my cousins' home and are smaller and darker than the usual peach we find at the grocer's. These cookies may be made with any jam or preserve, but they are a good excuse to seek out new, unusual flavors. A very chunky preserve should be roughly pureed first, using a food processor or food mill, to be the proper jamlike consistency for these cookies. The flaky sour cream pastry is enhanced with a bit of brown sugar. ¶The pinwheels are fun to make. When the tips of the cut-out dough are pulled to the center to form the pinwheels, be sure to press them in firmly or the cookies will open like flowers during baking.

2¼ cups all-purpose flour
½ teaspoon salt
¾ cup (1½ sticks) cold unsalted butter, cut into ¼-inch slices
1 large egg
½ cup sour cream
¼ cup firmly packed light brown sugar
About ½ cup Indian peach preserves or other thick jam

In a food processor, briefly pulse together the flour and salt. Scatter the butter over the flour mixture, and process just until the butter is blended and large crumbs appear. Transfer the mixture to a large bowl. Or, in a large bowl, whisk together the flour and salt. Scatter the butter over the flour mixture and cut it in with a pastry cutter until large crumbs start to form. ¶In a cup, whisk together the egg, sour cream, and brown sugar until well blended, and gradually stir it into the crumb mixture; combine well. Turn out the dough onto a lightly floured surface and knead a few times until smooth. Divide the dough in half and flatten each half slightly. Wrap tightly in plastic wrap and chill for 30 minutes. ¶Preheat the oven to 375° F. On a lightly floured surface, with a lightly floured rolling pin, roll the dough out to a 12- by 15-inch rectangle (patch as needed), about ⅛ inch thick. Lift or rotate the dough occasionally to check if it is sticking. Lightly reflour the work surface and the rolling pin as needed. Using a pastry wheel or knife, cut the dough into 3-inch squares. Place the squares 2 inches apart on ungreased baking sheets. On each square, make a diagonal cut from the tip of each corner halfway to the center. With your thumb or the back of a spoon, make a slight indentation in the center of each square and fill each indentation with one scant teaspoonful of jam. Pull the alternate tips of the square to the center and press very firmly in place. ¶Bake in the center of the oven for about 15 to 20 minutes, or until the pastry edges turn golden brown. Let the cookies cool on the baking sheet for a few minutes, then transfer them to a wire rack to cool completely. Store in an airtight container. Well-wrapped cookies may be frozen.

Makes about 2½ dozen cookies

ICEBOX COOKIES

Icebox cookies originated when the dough was stored in the old-time icebox; today they are also known as refrigerator cookies. The dough is rolled by hand into logs, wrapped in waxed paper or plastic wrap, and refrigerated until firm enough to slice. The dough may also be frozen (double-wrapped in freezer paper or aluminum foil for extra protection), but it should be partly thawed before slicing. A thin, sharp knife is best for cutting the cookies into slices.

Logs of icebox dough may vary in width and may be shaped into square-sided or triangular logs by pressing them with your hands. The dough can be rolled in such goodies as chopped nuts, colored sugar, or sprinkles so that, when sliced, the cookies will have a decorative edge.

With a cache of icebox cookie dough in your refrigerator or freezer, you can serve a spur-of-the-moment guest with warm, freshly baked cookies with little effort. Icebox cookie dough allows you to custom bake just the quantity you want—large or small. In fact, they are ideal for large parties because they can so easily be made in advance. For parties, small bite-sized cookies are nicer than large ones (roll the dough into narrow logs). Icebox dough can be stored for a few days in the refrigerator and in the freezer for up to 1 month.

VANILLA BEAN BUTTER COOKIES

The hundreds of tiny seeds inside the fragrant vanilla bean are the black specks in authentic vanilla-flavored products. Vanilla beans are available in the spice section of supermarkets and by mail. These double-vanilla cookies use both vanilla bean seeds and vanilla extract.

½ cup (1 stick) unsalted butter, softened
⅓ cup sugar
1 large egg yolk
One 2-inch piece vanilla bean, cut from the widest part
½ teaspoon pure vanilla extract
1 cup all-purpose flour
¼ teaspoon salt

In a large bowl, with an electric mixer on low speed, cream the butter and sugar together. Beat in the egg yolk. Place a spoonful of the butter mixture in a cup. Split the vanilla bean lengthwise, open it to expose the tiny seeds and, with a small spoon or blunt knife, scoop them out (clumped together they'll be about the size of a garden pea) and transfer to the spoonful of butter mixture; mix well. Add the vanilla bean mixture to the butter mixture and blend well. ¶In a small bowl, whisk together the flour and salt, and add to the butter mixture on low speed; combine well. Shape the dough into a log 9 inches long. Wrap in waxed paper or plastic wrap and twist the ends closed. Chill until firm, about 2 hours or overnight. ¶Preheat the oven to 350°F. Cut the chilled dough into ¼-inch-thick slices and place 1 inch apart on ungreased baking sheets. Bake in the center of the oven for about 12 to 15

minutes, or until the cookies are very light golden brown at the edges. Let the cookies cool on the baking sheet for a few minutes, then transfer them to a wire rack to cool completely. Store in an airtight container. Well-wrapped cookies may be frozen.

Makes about 3 dozen cookies

ZEBRA ICEBOX COOKIES

These vanilla and chocolate cookies are simple to make, despite their lovely marbleized effect. They add an elegant dimension to a tea tray and are a good choice to make as a gift when time is limited.

1 square (1 ounce) unsweetened chocolate
1½ cups all-purpose flour
¼ teaspoon salt
1 teaspoon baking powder
½ cup (1 stick) unsalted butter, softened
¾ cup sugar
1 large egg
1 teaspoon pure vanilla extract

Melt the chocolate in the top of a double boiler over barely simmering water; set aside to cool slightly. In a small bowl, whisk together the flour, salt, and baking powder; set aside. In a medium bowl, with an electric mixer on medium speed, cream the butter and sugar together. Mix in the egg and vanilla extract. On low speed, slowly add the flour mixture to the butter mixture and combine well. ¶Place one half of the dough on a sheet of waxed paper. Stir the cooled melted chocolate into the remaining half of the dough. Blend until the color is uniform. Scrape the chocolate dough onto the waxed paper alongside the vanilla dough and press the two together to form a ball. Knead just long enough to achieve a marbleized effect. Shape the dough into a 1-by 12-inch log. Wrap tightly in waxed paper or plastic wrap and twist the ends closed. Chill for 2 to 3 hours or until firm. ¶Preheat the oven to 375° F. Lightly grease the baking sheets. Cut the chilled dough into ¼-inch-thick slices and place 1 inch apart on the prepared baking sheets. Bake in the center of the oven for about 8 to 9 minutes, or until the cookies are set but not browned. Let the cookies cool on the baking sheet for a few minutes, then transfer them to a wire rack to cool completely. Store in an airtight container. Well-wrapped cookies may be frozen.

Makes about 3 dozen cookies

GRANDMOTHER NELLIE'S BUTTERSCOTCH ICEBOX COOKIES

This is Grandmother Nellie's recipe for a soft, plain cookie with a butterscotch flavor and a generous amount of pecans. She always cut her pecans into neat ¼-inch slices—a signature of sorts that I continue.

3½ cups all-purpose flour
1 teaspoon baking soda
½ teaspoon salt
1 cup (2 sticks) unsalted butter, softened
1 pound (2⅓ cups) firmly packed dark brown sugar
2 large eggs
1 teaspoon pure vanilla extract
1½ cups (6 ounces) pecans, sliced or chopped

In a medium bowl, whisk together the flour, baking soda, and salt; set aside. In a large bowl, with an electric mixer on low speed, cream the butter and brown sugar together until well blended. Mix in the eggs and vanilla extract. Gradually add the flour mixture and combine well. Mix in the sliced pecans. ¶Divide the dough in half and shape each into a log 1½ inches in diameter, on a sheet of waxed paper or plastic wrap. Roll and cover in the paper, twisting the ends closed. Chill the dough for several hours or overnight. ¶Preheat the oven to 350° F. Cut the chilled dough into ¼-inch-thick slices and place 1 inch apart on ungreased baking sheets. Bake in the center of the oven for about 8 minutes, or until the cookies are firm but not browned. Let the cookies cool on the baking sheet for a few minutes, then transfer them to a wire rack to cool completely. Store in an airtight container. Well-wrapped cookies may be frozen.

Makes about 3½ dozen cookies

MOCHA MACADAMIA SHORTBREAD

Australian in origin but widely cultivated in Hawaii, macadamia nuts have become a hit in the continental United States. Their texture is enticing, and their buttery flavor reminds me faintly of hazelnuts. Although these tender cookies have the sophisticated flavors of coffee and macadamia nuts, they appeal to people of all ages. My friend Carter has requested them since he was a young boy. The tawny mocha icing on the blond cookie adds even more flavor.

¾ cup (3½ ounces) salted macadamia nuts
⅔ cup sugar
½ teaspoon pure vanilla extract
1 cup (2 sticks) unsalted butter, cut into ½-inch pieces
2¼ cups all-purpose flour
Mocha Icing (recipe follows)

Place the macadamia nuts and sugar in a food processor; pulse for about 30 seconds, or until the mixture resembles cornmeal. Sprinkle the vanilla extract over the mixture and then scatter the butter. Process the mixture just until smooth. Add 1¼ cups of the flour to the macadamia mixture and pulse just until the flour is incorporated. Stir in the remaining cup of flour and process just until the dough starts to form a ball. Or, grind the nuts in a grinder or blender; set aside. In a medium bowl, with an electric mixer on low speed, beat the butter and sugar together; stir in the vanilla extract and ground nuts. Slowly add the flour and mix well. ¶Briefly knead the dough to fold in any loose crumbs. Divide the dough in half and shape each half into a log about 8 inches long on a sheet of waxed paper or plastic wrap. Wrap the waxed paper tightly around the dough and twist the ends closed. Chill for several hours or overnight. ¶Preheat the oven to 350°F. Cut the chilled dough into ⅓-inch-thick slices and place 1 inch apart on ungreased baking sheets. Bake in the center of the oven for about 8 to 9 minutes, or until just until set but not brown. Let the cookies cool on the baking sheet for a few minutes, then transfer them to a wire rack (take care in handling them, for they are somewhat fragile). ¶Glaze the cookies while still warm (the glaze will get an attractive sheen that way) with the mocha icing. Use a 1-inch pastry brush to ice the cookies, or a small spatula or the back of a spoon could be used instead. Store in an airtight container. Well-wrapped cookies may be frozen. Separate the cookies with sheets of waxed paper to prevent the glaze from sticking.

Makes about 4 dozen cookies

Mocha Icing
1 *tablespoon instant coffee granules*
3 *tablespoons boiling water*
4 *tablespoons (½ stick) butter, melted*
1¾ *cups confectioners' sugar, sifted*
1 *teaspoon pure vanilla extract*

Dissolve the coffee granules in the boiling water. Whisk in the melted butter, confectioners' sugar, and vanilla extract, mixing until smooth. Cover the icing with plastic wrap touching the icing surface until ready to use.

CORNMEAL COOKIES

Cornmeal is rarely used in cookies, but two exceptions are *gialetti*, Italian cookies made with polenta, a coarse-ground cornmeal (often lemon flavored and studded with currants) and *molletes*, Mexican cookies made with masa harina, a Mexican corn flour. ¶These distinctive cornmeal cookies have a uniquely pleasant, nutty flavor with a subtle scent of spice and a sandy texture. They are molded into a square-sided log and embossed with the tines of a fork.

1½ *cups all-purpose flour*
¾ *cup yellow cornmeal (preferably stone ground)*
¼ *teaspoon salt*
¼ *teaspoon ground nutmeg or ground cinnamon*
⅞ *cup (1¾ sticks) unsalted butter, softened*
¾ *cup sugar*
2 *large egg yolks*
1 *drop pure orange oil (optional)*

In a medium bowl, combine the flour, cornmeal, salt, and nutmeg; set aside. In a medium bowl, using a large wooden spoon, cream the butter and sugar together. Beat in the egg yolks and optional orange oil. Stir in the flour mixture. ¶Divide the dough in half and shape each portion into a 1¾- by 7-inch log on a sheet of waxed paper or plastic wrap. Flatten one log a bit by pressing it gently. Roll the log a quarter turn away from you and repeat 3 more times to form a square-sided log. Wrap tightly in waxed paper and twist the ends closed. Repeat with the remaining log. Chill for several hours or overnight. ¶Preheat the oven

to 350°F. Cut the chilled dough into ¼-inch-thick slices and place 1½ inches apart on ungreased baking sheets. Press the tines of a fork diagonally across each corner to decorate. ¶Bake in the center of the oven for about 12 to 15 minutes, or until the cookies are a very light golden brown at the edges. Let the cookies cool on the baking sheet for a few minutes, then transfer them to a wire rack to cool completely. Store in an airtight container. Well-wrapped cookies may be frozen.

Makes about 3½ dozen cookies

Crystallized Ginger Logs

It is difficult to say no to these contemporary-looking cookies studded with fiery bits of crystallized ginger. This is a recipe for those who love ginger. I like to serve these with green tea after an Asian meal.

1¾ cups all-purpose flour
½ teaspoon baking powder
¼ teaspoon ground ginger
¼ teaspoon salt
½ cup (1 stick) unsalted butter, softened
⅔ cup sugar
1 large egg
½ teaspoon pure vanilla extract
⅔ cup coarsely chopped crystallized ginger

In a medium bowl, whisk together the flour, baking powder, ground ginger, and salt; set aside. In a large bowl, with an electric mixer on low speed, cream the butter and sugar together until pale in color. Mix in the egg and vanilla extract. Gradually add the flour mixture and mix well. Stir in the crystallized ginger. Flatten dough into a round about 1½ inches thick. The edges will be uneven. Wrap in plastic wrap and chill for 1 hour or until firm. ¶Preheat the oven to 350°F. Cut the round of dough (as if slicing a round loaf of bread) into ¼-inch-thick slices (they will be different lengths) and place them 2 inches apart on ungreased baking sheets, flat side down. ¶Bake in the center of the oven for about 10 minutes, or until the cookies are a light golden brown at the edges. Let the cookies cool on the baking sheet for a few minutes, then transfer them to a wire rack to cool completely. Store in an airtight container. Well-wrapped cookies may be frozen.

Makes about 3 dozen cookies

MOLDED COOKIES

Molded cookies are eye-catching and rewarding to do if you are not in a rush. They usually require extra equipment. Various molds, tartlet pans, cookie presses, and krumkake irons are available at baking supply stores, gourmet cookware stores, and by mail. I've found a few goodies at garage sales and flea markets.

Shortbread cookies can be baked in molded baking pans (usually metal or ceramic) or the dough can be pressed into wooden molds (or other materials) before baking, turned out on a baking sheet and baked. The type of mold will usually dictate its use. Molds of both types should be lightly floured or oiled (or both, depending on the mold) so that the dough will unmold. I often bake shortbread in a round cake pan or a decoratively shaped baking pan and unmold it after baking.

Madeleines are baked in unique shell-shaped pans. Different sizes are available, and the various sized madeleines make a beautiful presentation. Shortbread also can be molded or baked in madeleine molds.

Tartlets are baked in tiny, beautifully shaped pans placed on a baking sheet. They may be baked with or without their filling, depending on the recipe.

Scandinavian krumkake irons and Italian pizzelle irons produce delicate, crisp, embossed wafers. The irons are available in easy-to-use electric models (my preference), as well as old-fashioned hand-held models that are used on the top of a stove over a burner.

Spritz cookies are molded with a cookie press (or gun). The sturdy metal presses are more expensive and more durable than the plastic models. They come with interchangeable discs of different designs. It takes a little practice to press out the desired amount of dough, but this trick is easy to master.

Biscotti are hand molded into large logs, baked, cut into slices, and baked again for their characteristic toasted look and dry texture.

PISTACHIO BUTTERBALLS

Pale green pistachios star in this tender, easy-to-make cookie. Substitute other nuts such as hickory nuts or the native American butternut, also known as the white walnut, both available by mail.

½ cup (1 stick) unsalted butter, softened
¼ cup sugar
¾ teaspoon pure vanilla extract
2 tablespoons honey
1 cup all-purpose flour
¼ teaspoon salt
¾ cup (4 ounces) unsalted pistachios, finely chopped

Preheat the oven to 325°F. In a medium bowl, with an electric mixer on low speed, cream the butter, sugar, vanilla extract, and honey together. Mix the flour and salt together, and add gradually to the butter mixture. Stir in the pistachios. ¶Shape the dough into 1½-inch balls and place them 2 inches apart on ungreased cookie sheets. Bake in the center of the oven for about 12 to 14 minutes, or until the cookies are set but not brown. Let the cookies cool on the baking sheet for a few minutes, then transfer them to a wire rack to cool completely. Store in an airtight container. Well-wrapped cookies may be frozen.

Makes about 1½ dozen cookies

PEANUT BUTTER THUMBPRINTS

A peanut butter version of a classic American cookie is rolled in chopped peanuts and indented to fill with thick jam such as apricot, blackberry, or strawberry jam. Don't use jellies or honey; they are too thin and will melt out of the cookie.

1¼ cups all-purpose flour
¼ teaspoon salt
⅛ teaspoon ground cinnamon
½ cup (1 stick) unsalted butter, softened
⅓ cup sugar
¼ cup creamy peanut butter
1 large egg, separated
½ teaspoon pure vanilla extract
¾ cup (3½ ounces) salted or unsalted peanuts, chopped
1 cup jam

Preheat the oven to 375° F. In a small bowl, whisk together the flour, salt, and cinnamon; set aside. In a medium bowl, with an electric mixer on low speed, cream the butter and sugar together. Mix in the peanut butter, egg yolk, and vanilla extract. Blend the flour mixture into the peanut butter mixture. ¶Shape the dough into 1-inch balls. In a small bowl, lightly beat the egg white a few strokes until frothy. Dip each ball in the egg white, then roll in chopped peanuts to cover the surface. Place the balls 1½ inches apart on ungreased baking sheets. Press your thumb or a thimble into the center of each cookie and fill each cookie with a teaspoonful of jam. ¶Bake in the center of the oven for about 10 to 12 minutes, or until lightly brown. Let cookies cool on the baking sheet for a few minutes, then transfer them to a wire rack to cool completely. Store in an airtight container. Well-wrapped cookies may be frozen.

Makes about 3 dozen cookies

CAPPUCCINO CREAMS

These sophisticated cookies are scented with coffee, molded into the shape of coffee beans, and sandwiched together with a cinnamon filling. They are good with a cup of coffee or cappuccino, or a glass of milk.

2 teaspoons instant coffee granules
1 teaspoon boiling water
1 cup (2 sticks) unsalted butter, softened
⅔ cup firmly packed light brown sugar
1 large egg yolk
2 cups all-purpose flour
Cinnamon Filling (recipe follows)

Preheat the oven to 325° F. In a cup, dissolve the coffee granules in the boiling water. In a medium bowl, with an electric mixer on low speed, cream the butter and brown sugar together. Add the egg yolk and coffee. Add the flour gradually, mixing until well blended. ¶With lightly floured hands, pinch off the dough into ¾-inch balls. Roll the balls into oval shapes between your palms or on a floured surface. Briefly roll the ends of each log to narrow them into points. Place the ovals 2 inches apart on ungreased baking sheets. On each cookie use the back of a table knife to press a lengthwise indentation, moderately deep, to give the look of a coffee bean. ¶Bake in the center of the oven for about 10 to 12 minutes, or until set but not browned. Let the cookies cool on the baking sheet for a few minutes, then transfer them to a wire rack to cool completely. Store the unfilled cookies in an airtight container or freeze them; sandwich the cookies together with the icing a few hours before serving. ¶To fill: Make the cinnamon filling. Spread a ¼-inch layer of cinnamon filling on the bottom side of a flat cookie. Top with an indented cookie, with the flat side touching the filling, and press gently together. Repeat with the remaining cookies and filling.

Makes about 3 dozen sandwich cookies

Cinnamon Filling
1½ cups confectioners' sugar, sifted
½ teaspoon ground cinnamon
¼ teaspoon salt
4 tablespoons (½ stick) unsalted butter, melted
1 teaspoon coffee liqueur or pure vanilla extract
2 to 3 tablespoons half-and-half or milk

In a medium bowl, whisk together the confectioners' sugar, cinnamon, and salt. Stir in the melted butter, coffee liqueur or vanilla extract, and 2 tablespoons of the half-and-half or milk. Mix to blend well. The filling should be creamy and easily spreadable. If it is too thick, thin with half-and-half, 1 teaspoon at a time.

Grand Marnier Balls

Grand Marnier flavors these heady no-bake cookies that are favorites for the holidays. Make them several days ahead so that the flavors can ripen. For a selection of cookies, substitute different liqueurs for the Grand Marnier, such as Amaretto, Tia Maria, and crème de menthe. To prepare cookie crumbs, see the directions on page 24.

2 cups sugar cookie crumbs, preferably from homemade cookies
1 cup (4 ounces) pecans, finely chopped
1 cup confectioners' sugar, sifted
2 tablespoons unsweetened cocoa
1 tablespoon butter, melted
¼ cup cane sugar syrup (golden syrup) or light corn syrup
⅓ cup Grand Marnier or other liqueur
Sifted confectioners' sugar for coating

In a large bowl, with a wooden spoon, mix together the cookie crumbs, pecans, 1 cup confectioners' sugar, cocoa, butter, and cane sugar syrup. Add the Grand Marnier or other liqueur, stirring to blend well. ¶Shape into 1-inch balls with a small ice cream scoop, 2 spoons, or your palms. Roll in confectioners' sugar (granulated sugar, chocolate sprinkles, or finely chopped nuts may be substituted). Place on a sheet of waxed paper to dry for 2 to 3 hours. Store different flavors separately in airtight containers. Well-wrapped cookies may be frozen. Make the cookies at least several days ahead to allow the flavors to ripen.

Makes about 3 dozen balls

Molasses Pirouettes

Pirouettes are made by rolling warm cookies over the handle of a large wooden spoon or a ½-inch wooden dowel. The secret is to bake and roll just 2 or 3 cookies at a time. The elegant flutes may be served plain or try filling them with delicately sweetened and flavored whipped cream just before serving, so that they remain crisp.

½ *cup (1 stick) unsalted butter*
½ *cup unsulfured molasses*
3 *tablespoons sugar*
1 *cup all-purpose flour*
¼ *teaspoon salt*
¼ *teaspoon ground cinnamon*
¼ *teaspoon ground ginger*
¼ *teaspoon ground cloves*

Preheat the oven to 350°F. Grease the baking sheets or line them with aluminum foil. In a medium saucepan over medium heat, melt the butter, molasses, and sugar. Remove from the heat, sift the flour, salt, cinnamon, ginger, and cloves over the molasses mixture; blend well. Place the saucepan over the lowest heat possible to keep the dough warm or it will become too thick to use properly. Drop the dough by rounded teaspoonfuls 3 inches apart on the prepared baking sheet. The cookies will spread. ¶Bake in the center of the oven for about 7 to 8 minutes, or until bubbly. Let the cookies cool on the baking sheet for exactly 1 minute. The first cookie will be quite hot. Roll the cookie around a wooden spoon handle, overlapping the cookie to make a cylinder, and press down on the seam for a few seconds to seal the shape. Let the cookies cool on a wire rack. Repeat with the remaining cookies. Store in an airtight container.

Makes about 2 dozen cookies

HIGHLAND SHORTBREAD

Authentic Scottish shortbread is simplicity itself and should be made with top-quality ingredients. Along with all-purpose flour, this recipe uses rice flour for flavor and crispness. It is available in natural foods stores and some grocery stores and may be kept in the refrigerator or freezer (in an airtight container) for months. Another ingredient is vanilla sugar, often used by European cooks. ¶This is probably the quickest recipe in the book and an excellent choice for a last-minute cookie, especially if baked in a pan and then unmolded.

1¾ *cups all-purpose flour*
¼ *cup rice flour, preferably brown*
½ *cup vanilla sugar (see page 24), or ½ cup sugar plus ¾ teaspoon*
   pure vanilla extract
½ *teaspoon salt*
1 *cup (2 sticks) unsalted butter, cut into ¼-inch slices*

Preheat the oven to 325°F. In a food processor, blend the flour, rice flour, vanilla sugar, and salt with a few short pulses. Scatter the butter slices over the flour mixture and process briefly until the mixture starts to clump together. Or, in a medium bowl, whisk together the flour, rice flour, vanilla sugar or sugar and vanilla extract, and salt. Cut the butter into the flour mixture with a pastry cutter. Knead by hand a moment to gather in loose crumbs. ¶Press the dough into an 8-inch round cake or pie pan. The shortbread can be baked directly in the cake pan or unmolded onto a baking sheet if you like. To unmold the shortbread, place an ungreased baking sheet on top of the pan, hold both firmly, and flip them over. A tap or two may be needed to release the shortbread. Score the surface into 8 or 12 wedges using a knife and decorate it by pricking with a fork. Flute the edges with your

fingertips. Cover and chill the shortbread for 10 to 15 minutes (lightly covered) to help the shortbread hold its shape and decorative marks during baking. If you wish to use a traditional Scottish wooden mold, lightly flour it and press the dough firmly into the mold; level the surface. To unmold the dough, turn the mold over a baking sheet and tap the mold with the heel of your hand (at different points if necessary) to release the dough. ¶Bake the shortbread in the center of the oven for about 20 to 30 minutes, or until golden brown around edges. Let the shortbread cool on the baking sheet or in the pan for about 10 minutes. Cut into wedges on the scored lines, then transfer to a wire rack to cool completely. Store in an airtight container. Well-wrapped shortbread may be frozen.

BOURBON PECAN CRESCENTS

Bourbon and pecans always remind me of the South because they are so often used in Southern cooking and because pecans are native to the United States. Many people know the wonderful papershell pecans, but there are smaller, delicious wild pecans also, available by mail. ¶Here, rich pecan shortbread is baked into the shape of crescents and given a heady bourbon glaze or dusted with confectioners' sugar.

1 cup (4 ounces) pecans
1¼ cup sugar
½ cup firmly packed dark brown sugar
1 cup (2 sticks) unsalted butter, cut into ¼-inch slices
1 teaspoon pure vanilla extract
½ teaspoon salt
2¼ cups all-purpose flour
Bourbon Glaze (recipe follows) or sifted confectioners' sugar

Preheat the oven to 350°F. In a food processor, combine the pecans, sugar, and brown sugar; pulse until the pecans are coarsely ground. Scatter the butter over the nut mixture and process briefly. Add the vanilla extract and salt. Pulse until the mixture looks uniform and the butter is blended. Add about half of the flour and pulse just until the flour is incorporated. Add the remaining flour and pulse just until the flour is blended and the mixture starts to form a ball. Or, grind the pecans in a blender or nut grinder and set aside. In a medium bowl, with an electric mixer on low speed, beat the sugar, brown sugar, and butter until creamy. Add the vanilla extract and salt. Stir in the pecans. Gradually add the flour and combine well. ¶Shape the dough into 1¼-inch balls. Roll each ball on a lightly floured surface to form a small log 3 inches long and tapered at each end. ¶Place on an ungreased baking sheet and shape into a crescent. Repeat with the remaining dough, spacing the cookies 1 inch apart. ¶Bake in the center of the oven for about 13 to 15 minutes, or until set but not browned. Let the cookies cool on the baking sheet for a few minutes, then transfer them to a wire rack to cool completely. Prepare the bourbon glaze, if using. Using a pastry brush, ice the crescents with the bourbon glaze, or dust them with confectioners' sugar. Store in an airtight container. Well-wrapped cookies may be frozen

Makes about 3½ dozen cookies

Bourbon Glaze
5 tablespoons unsalted butter
2 tablespoons bourbon or milk
1½ cups confectioners' sugar, sifted

In a medium saucepan, lightly brown the butter. Remove from the heat, stir in the bourbon or milk and confectioners' sugar. Blend until smooth. Use the glaze while warm.

ALMOND MADELEINES

Classic French madeleines are pretty, shell-shaped cakes baked in special molded pans. I prefer to use natural, unblanched almonds for this recipe rather than blanched because, when ground, they add attractive brown flecks to the madeleines. The flavor of these madeleines is so good that I often give them as gifts, beautifully packaged.

6 tablespoons (¾ stick) unsalted butter
¾ cup (5 ounces) natural, unblanched whole almonds
⅔ cup sugar
½ cup all-purpose flour
¼ teaspoon salt
4 large egg whites
½ teaspoon pure almond extract

Preheat the oven to 400°F. Generously butter or grease the shell portions of the madeleine pans. In a small saucepan, melt the butter over medium heat, browning it lightly for extra flavor. In a food processor, pulse the almonds and sugar together until the almonds are ground. Don't overprocess or they will turn to nut butter. Place the sugar-almond mixture in a medium bowl. Or, grind the nuts in a hand grinder or blender and mix with the sugar in a medium bowl. ¶Using a wooden spoon, stir the flour and salt into the almond-sugar mixture. Whisk in the egg whites and almond extract and blend well. Slowly add the melted butter while stirring the batter with the whisk. Transfer the batter to a glass measuring cup or a small pitcher and pour the batter directly into each shell, filling each three fourths full. ¶Bake in the center of the oven for about 12 to 15 minutes, or until well browned around the edges. Let cool in the pans for 1 or 2 minutes, then turn the pans over a wire rack to release the madeleines to cool completely. Store in an airtight container. Well-wrapped madeleines may be frozen.

Makes about eighteen 3-inch madeleines

DARK CHOCOLATE MADELEINES

These dark beauties, with their glossy chocolate icing, are luxurious. Serve them on your finest dishes.

⅓ cup all-purpose flour
¼ cup Dutch process unsweetened cocoa
⅛ teaspoon baking powder
¼ teaspoon salt
1 large egg
⅓ cup sugar
½ teaspoon instant coffee granules
1 teaspoon pure vanilla extract
4 tablespoons (½ stick) unsalted butter, melted
Chocolate Glaze (recipe follows)

Preheat the oven to 350°F. Grease and flour the madeleine pan. In a small bowl, whisk together the flour, cocoa, baking powder, and salt; set aside. In a medium bowl, whisk together the egg, sugar, coffee granules, and vanilla extract. Slowly whisk in the butter. Gradually stir the flour mixture into the sugar mixture. Transfer the batter to a glass measuring cup or a small pitcher. Pour the batter directly into each shell, filling each three fourths

full. ¶Bake in the center of the oven for about 15 to 20 minutes, or until the madeleines spring back when lightly touched. Let the madeleines cool for a minute or two, then turn the pan over a wire rack to release the madeleines to cool completely. Make the chocolate glaze. Brush the warm glaze on the madeleines with a pastry brush. Let cool and store in an airtight container.

Makes about twelve 3-inch madeleines

Chocolate Glaze
2 tablespoons butter
2 squares (2 ounces) semisweet chocolate, chopped

In the top of a double boiler over barely simmering water, melt the butter and chocolate, stirring until melted and smooth. Use the glaze warm.

JAM TARTS

Delicious, colorful jam tarts are a British treat served, even in the remotest campsites of Kenya, at teatime. Bake the dough in decorative tartlet pans or in muffin pans. Fill the dough with high-quality jams in a palette of colors and flavors. Try flavors such as pineapple-ginger preserves, quince jelly, lemon marmalade, and huckleberry jam.

1 cup all-purpose flour
½ teaspoon salt
1 tablespoon sugar
6 tablespoons (¾ stick) cold unsalted butter, cut into ¼-inch slices
1 to 2 tablespoons ice water
¼ teaspoon pure vanilla extract
About ½ cup preserves, jelly, marmalade, or jam

Place the flour, salt, and sugar in a food processor and pulse to combine. Scatter the butter slices over the flour mixture. Process just until the mixture forms large crumbs. Evenly sprinkle 1 tablespoon of ice water over the crumbs. Process just until dough starts to form a ball. Add more water if needed, 1 teaspoon at a time. Or, in a medium bowl, whisk together the flour, salt, and sugar. Scatter the butter slices over the flour mixture. Cut the butter in with a pastry cutter until the mixture forms large crumbs. Sprinkle 1 tablespoon of water over the crumbs and mix just until the dough starts to come together. Add more water if needed, 1 teaspoon at a time. Wrap the dough well in plastic wrap and chill for 30 minutes. ¶Preheat the oven to 425° F. On a lightly floured surface, with a lightly floured rolling pin, roll the dough ⅛ inch thick. If using tartlet pans, lightly grease them and place them upside down on the dough, cutting a 1-inch border around each with a knife. Press the dough into the pans and trim off dough with a thumb. Or, group the pans and run a rolling pin firmly on top to trim them all at once. Place the tartlets 1 inch apart on a baking sheet; fill each half full with jam or jelly. Or, cut six 2½-inch rounds of dough to fit into the bottoms (and ¼-inch up the sides) of 6 lightly greased muffin cups. Fill each muffin tart half full with jam or jelly. ¶Bake in the center of the oven for about 10 minutes, or until the pastry is lightly browned at edges and the jam or jelly is melted. Don't underbake. Let the tarts cool completely, then gently remove them from the pans. Store in an airtight container.

Makes about six 2½-inch tartlets, depending on the shape

SUMMER BERRY TARTLETS

In the height of summer, when I lived on Berry Road, I made large tarts using three kinds of berries together: raspberries, blackberries, and blueberries. The depth of color in these tartlets is extraordinary and the flavor is wildly delicious. This is a dreamy dessert for a midsummer's night.

Dough
½ cup (2½ ounces) almonds, ground
¼ cup sugar
½ cup (1 stick) cold unsalted butter, cut into ¼-inch slices
1½ cups all-purpose flour
2 to 3 tablespoons ice water

Cream Cheese Filling
12 ounces cream cheese, softened
¾ cup superfine sugar
1 tablespoon fresh lemon juice
1 teaspoon pure vanilla extract

Berry Topping
1 pint (2 cups) fresh blueberries
½ pint (1 cup) fresh red raspberries
½ pint (1 cup) fresh blackberries
⅔ cup sugar
2 tablespoons cornstarch
3 tablespoons water

To make the dough: In a food processor, pulse the almonds and sugar together just until the almonds are finely ground. Don't overprocess or the mixture may turn to nut butter. Add the butter and pulse to blend. Add 1 cup of the flour and process just until the flour is incorporated. Add the remaining ½ cup of flour and pulse just until the mixture forms large crumbs. Sprinkle 2 tablespoons of ice water over the mixture. Process, adding more water if needed, 1 teaspoon at a time, just until the mixture starts to form a ball. Or, grind the almonds in a nut grinder or blender; set aside. In a medium bowl, using a pastry cutter, cut the butter into the flour until large crumbs appear. Stir in the almonds and sugar, blending well. Sprinkle 2 tablespoons of ice water over the mixture. Mix well, adding more water if needed, a teaspoon at a time, until a ball of dough can be formed. Wrap the dough tightly in plastic wrap and chill for 30 minutes. ¶Preheat the oven to 350° F. On a lightly floured board, with a lightly floured rolling pin, roll out the dough ⅛ inch thick. Lightly grease the tartlet pans and place them upside down on the dough. Cut a 1-inch border around each pan. Turn the pans right side up and press the dough into each pan. Trim the excess dough with your thumb or group the tartlet pans and run a rolling pin over them to trim all at once. Place the tartlet pans 1 inch apart on a baking sheet (they are baked unfilled) Prick bottoms with a fork. ¶Bake in the center of the oven for about 15 to 20 minutes, or until light brown at edges. Let the tartlet shells cool completely, then gently remove the fragile shells from the pans. ¶To make the filling: In a medium bowl, with an electric mixer on medium speed, mix all the ingredients until creamy; cover and set aside. ¶To make the berry topping: In a medium bowl, gently mix the berries together. In a medium saucepan, blend the sugar and cornstarch. Add the water and half of the berries. Cook over medium heat, stirring with a wooden spoon, until the mixture thickens, about 5 minutes. Set aside to cool, uncovered. ¶Divide the cream cheese filling evenly among the tartlet shells. Spoon the cooked berry topping over the filling and top with the reserved mixed fresh berries. Cover with plastic wrap and refrigerate until serving. The pastry shells may be made in advance and frozen. The filled tartlets will soften a little upon standing, so fill them no more than 4 hours before serving them.

Makes about eight 4-inch tartlets

CARDAMOM WAFERS

Cardamom adds to the appeal of these crisp embossed wafers, which are quickly made with a pizzelle or krumkake iron. These are nice to make in the summertime because the oven doesn't have to be used and because the attractive wafers are a good complement to frosty summer desserts. I often give them as gifts because they are such a change of pace.

1 cup all-purpose flour
⅛ teaspoon baking powder
½ teaspoon ground cardamom
⅛ teaspoon salt
⅓ cup sugar
1 large egg
4 tablespoons (½ stick) unsalted butter, melted
½ teaspoon pure lemon extract

On the top of a stove, preheat a hand-held krumkake or pizzelle iron for about 5 minutes per side over medium heat, or follow the manufacturer's instructions for preheating electric models. Use a vegetable-oil spray to oil the iron if it isn't seasoned. ¶In a small bowl, whisk together the flour, baking powder, cardamom, and salt; set aside. In a medium bowl, whisk the sugar and egg together until pale in color. Slowly whisk in the melted butter and lemon extract. Gradually add the flour mixture to the sugar mixture and combine well. The dough will be stiff. ¶The iron is ready when a drop of water sizzles as it hits the inside surface. To make 3-inch wafers, use a 1¼-inch scoop or a teaspoon to place a 1¼-inch ball of dough in the center of each plate. For larger wafers, use a larger ball of dough. Experiment to find just the right size for your iron for the results you want. Immediately close the iron (and clamp, if there is one) and cook for 25 to 30 seconds, or until browned. Use tongs or two forks, one on top

and one underneath, to quickly slide the wafer to a wire rack. Store in an airtight container. Well-wrapped wafers may be frozen.

Makes about 16 wafers

CHOCOLATE WAFERS

These delicate chocolate wafers are quick to make with a pizzelle or krumkake iron. The embossed wafers may be cut in halves or quarters while still warm. To turn a scoop of ice cream, frozen yogurt, or sorbet into dessert, place it in a stemmed glass or pretty dish, drizzle with pureed fruit, liqueur, or caramel sauce, and top with a chocolate wafer quarter.

1 cup all-purpose flour
2 tablespoons unsweetened cocoa
⅛ teaspoon salt
½ cup sugar
1 large egg
5 tablespoons unsalted butter, melted
1¼ teaspoons pure vanilla extract

On the top of a stove, preheat a hand-held krumkake or pizzelle iron for about 5 minutes per side over medium heat, or follow the manufacturer's instructions for preheating electric models. Use a vegetable-oil spray to oil the iron if it isn't seasoned. ¶In a small bowl, whisk together the flour, cocoa, and salt; set aside. In a medium bowl, whisk the sugar and egg together until pale in color. Slowly whisk in the melted butter and vanilla extract. Gradually add the flour mixture to the sugar mixture and combine well. The dough will be stiff. ¶The iron is ready when a drop of water sizzles as it hits the inside surface. To make 3-inch wafers, use a 1¼-inch scoop or a teaspoon to place a 1¼-inch ball

of dough in the center of each plate. For larger wafers, use a larger ball of dough. Experiment to find the best size for your iron. Immediately close the iron (and clamp, if there is one) and cook for 25 to 30 seconds, or until browned. Use tongs or two forks, one on top and one underneath, to quickly slide the wafer to a wire rack. Store in an airtight container. Well-wrapped wafers may be frozen.

Makes about 18 wafers

Old-fashioned Ice Cream Cones

With a krumkake or pizzelle iron, make your own authentic-tasting, old-fashioned ice cream cones—a perfect foil for your own homemade ice cream. To shape the hot wafers into cones, a wooden or metal cone (or cream-horn form) is helpful to make symmetrical cones, and is available at baking supply houses and by mail. (I prefer the wooden form because it doesn't get hot.) Cones can also be rolled free form or shaped around a homemade cone form made from recycled aluminum foil. It is best to make the cones one at a time.

½ cup all-purpose flour
⅛ teaspoon salt
½ cup firmly packed dark brown sugar
1 large egg
4 tablespoons (½ stick) unsalted butter, melted
1½ teaspoons pure vanilla extract
¼ teaspoon pure almond extract
About 1 pint ice cream

On the top of a stove, preheat a hand-held krumkake or pizzelle iron for about 5 minutes per side over medium heat, or follow the manufacturer's instructions for preheating electric models. Use a vegetable-oil spray to oil the iron if it isn't seasoned. ¶In a small bowl, whisk together the flour and salt; set aside. In a medium bowl, whisk the brown sugar and egg together until creamy. Slowly whisk in the melted butter, vanilla extract, and almond extract. Gradually add the flour mixture to the sugar mixture and combine well. The dough will be stiff. ¶The iron is ready when a drop of water sizzles as it hits the inside surface. To make 5-inch wafers for the cones, use a scoop or a spoon to place a 1⅜-inch ball of dough in the center of each plate. Immediately close the iron (and clamp, if there is one) and cook for 25 to 30 seconds, or until browned. Use tongs or 2 forks, one on top and one underneath, to quickly slide the wafer to a wire rack. Immediately wrap the hot wafer around the cone form (or roll into a free-form cone shape) and press the cone, seam side down, on a counter for about 15 seconds, or until the shape has set and the form can be removed. Repeat with the remaining wafers. Store in an airtight container. Well-wrapped cones may be frozen, filled or unfilled, but they will be slightly less crisp.

Makes about 8 ice cream cones

Variation
Ice Cream Sandwiches: Make 3-inch wafers for the ice cream sandwiches using 1¼-inch scoops of dough. Use a small ice cream scoop or spoon to make several small balls of ice cream and place on a wafer. Top with another wafer and press down gently (the wafers are brittle). The ice cream will soften slightly as you work, which will make it a little easier to assemble the sandwiches. Freeze ice cream sandwiches well wrapped. Makes about 6 ice cream sandwiches.

CASHEW SPRITZ

Cashew spritz are made with a cookie press. A handsome design is made with a "bar" disc, which looks like a buttonhole with one zigzag edge and makes a strip of dough with a textured surface.

¾ cup (1½ sticks) unsalted butter, softened
½ cup sugar
1 egg yolk
½ teaspoon pure vanilla extract
¼ cup (1¼ ounces) cashews, ground
1½ cups all-purpose flour
About 40 cashew halves for garnish

Preheat the oven to 375°F. In a medium bowl, with an electric mixer on medium speed, cream the butter and sugar together. Add the egg yolk, vanilla extract, and ground cashews. On low speed, gradually beat in the flour and mix until smooth. ¶To use a cookie press, pull the plunger back as far as it can go, close to the handle (some models have a button that has to be pressed to do this). Screw the body into the base near the handle. Fill the cookie press with spoonfuls of dough, filling it solidly up to the brim. Place the bar disc on top and screw on the outer ring. ¶Hold the cookie press at an approximate 45-degree angle to an ungreased baking sheet. Squeezing the handle in a continuous pumping motion, form a long cookie down the middle of the cookie sheet to within ½ inch of the top and bottom edges of the pan. Squeeze out parallel long cookies at least 1 inch from either side of the middle cookie. Use a long knife to cut the dough into triangles or squares. Do not separate the cookies. Top each cookie with a cashew piece pressed in halfway. ¶Bake in the center of the oven for about 8 to 9 minutes, or until set. Let the cookies cool on the baking sheet for a few minutes, then separate the cookies with a knife or pancake turner and transfer them to a wire rack to cool completely. Store in an airtight container. Well-wrapped cookies may be frozen.

Makes about 3½ dozen cookies

VANILLA BUTTER SPRITZ

When I think of spritz cookies, these dainty vanilla butter cookies with a top note of almond flavoring come to mind. They are suitable for all seasons, and may be dressed up with a cherry during the holidays.

1½ cups (3 sticks) unsalted butter, softened
⅞ cup (¾ cup plus 2 tablespoons) superfine or granulated sugar
2 tablespoons firmly packed light brown sugar
2 egg yolks
2 teaspoons pure vanilla extract
1 teaspoon pure almond extract
3½ cups all-purpose flour

Preheat the oven to 375°F. In a medium bowl, with an electric mixer on medium speed, cream the butter, superfine sugar, and brown sugar together. Add the egg yolks, vanilla extract, and almond extract. On low speed, gradually beat in the flour and mix until smooth. ¶To use a cookie press, pull the plunger back as far as it can go, close to the handle (some models have a button that has to be pressed to do this). Screw the body into the base near the handle. Fill the cookie press with spoonfuls of dough, filling it solidly up to the brim. Place the bar disc on top and screw on the outer ring. ¶Hold the cookie press upright, resting it on an ungreased baking sheet. Squeeze the handle to form a cookie, release the trigger, and lift up the cookie press. Most cookies may

need more than one squeeze. With a little practice for each disc (some take more pressure than others), it will be easy to figure out the size you want. Repeat until all the dough is used. ¶Bake in the center of the oven for about 8 to 9 minutes, or until set. Let the cookies cool on the baking sheet for a few minutes, then transfer them to a wire rack to cool completely. Store in an airtight container. Well-wrapped cookies may be frozen.

Makes about 5 dozen cookies

Bittersweet Chocolate Nut Biscotti

These biscotti have a flavor reminiscent of brownies. Dip each one in melted chocolate for extra luxury; see the recipe for Chocolate Undercoating on page 40. The whole nuts are beautiful in these cookies. Use a very sharp serrated knife to slice the biscotti with a gentle sawing motion—this cuts through the nuts without pulling them out of the cookie.

½ cup (1 stick) unsalted butter

4 squares (4 ounces) semisweet chocolate, finely chopped

½ cup unsweetened cocoa (preferably Dutch process)

1½ cups all-purpose flour

1½ teaspoons baking powder

½ teaspoon salt

¼ teaspoon ground cinnamon

1 cup sugar

2 large eggs

1 teaspoon pure vanilla extract

2 teaspoons rum or coffee liqueur (optional)

⅔ cup (3 ounces) whole Brazil nuts or macadamia nuts

Preheat the oven to 350°F. Grease and flour a large baking sheet. In the top of a double boiler over barely simmering water, melt the butter and chocolate together, stirring until smooth. Set aside to cool a few minutes. ¶In a medium bowl, whisk together the cocoa, flour, baking powder, salt, and cinnamon; set aside. In a large bowl, with an electric mixer on medium speed, beat the sugar and eggs together until pale in color. Add the vanilla extract and rum or coffee liqueur. On low speed, gradually beat in the chocolate mixture. Slowly add the flour mixture. With a wooden spoon, stir in the nuts. ¶Briefly knead the dough to gather in loose crumbs. Divide the dough in half. Form 2 smooth, somewhat flat 10-inch logs directly on the baking sheet. Smooth over the tops to cover the nuts, if necessary. ¶Bake in the center of the oven for 30 minutes, or until firm. Let cool on the baking sheet for 15 minutes. Transfer the logs to a cutting board and cut into ½-inch-thick diagonal slices, using a serrated knife and a gentle sawing motion. The loaves will be crumbly. ¶Place the slices, cut side down, close together on the baking sheet and bake for 7 minutes. Turn the slices over and bake 7 minutes longer. Let the biscotti cool on the baking sheet. If you want extra crunch, bake the cookies a few extra minutes longer on each side, but don't let them burn. Transfer to a wire rack to cool completely. Store in an airtight container. Well-wrapped biscotti may be frozen.

Makes about 3½ dozen cookies

TUSCAN BISCOTTINI

Biscottini are smaller versions of biscotti, and these are superb to serve after an Italian meal, with fresh fruit. The enticing bouquet of almonds, honey, and a nuance of spice in these cookies were inspired by the legendary biscotti of Tuscany. Use a very sharp serrated knife to cut the biscottini.

¾ cup (3¾ ounces) whole blanched almonds
⅓ cup raisins
1 tablespoon Cognac (optional)
2¼ cups all-purpose flour
½ teaspoon each baking powder and baking soda
½ teaspoon ground cinnamon
¼ teaspoon each ground allspice, ground mace, and salt
½ cup (1 stick) unsalted butter, softened
⅔ cup sugar
¼ cup honey
2 large eggs
½ teaspoon pure vanilla extract
½ teaspoon pure almond extract

Preheat the oven to 350°F. Grease and flour the baking sheets. Toast the almonds in a shallow pan in the center of the oven for about 10 minutes; let cool. Grind ¼ cup of the nuts in a food processor, blender, or nut grinder. Soak the raisins in the Cognac until ready to use, if desired. ¶In a medium bowl, whisk together the flour, ground almonds, baking powder, baking soda, cinnamon, allspice, mace, and salt; set aside. In a large bowl with an electric mixer on medium speed, cream the butter, sugar, and honey together. Beat in the eggs, vanilla extract, and almond extract. On low speed, gradually add flour mixture to the butter mixture. Combine well. Stir in almonds and raisins (drained). ¶Divide the dough into fourths. Shape each portion of dough into a long, somewhat flat 14-inch log, and place them 2 inches apart on the prepared baking sheets. ¶Bake in the center of the oven for about 20 minutes, or until golden brown. Let cool on the baking sheet for 10 minutes. Place one log on a cutting board. With a serrated knife, cut ⅜-inch-thick diagonal slices using a gentle sawing motion. Place the biscottini, cut side down, ½ inch apart on the baking sheets. Repeat with the 3 remaining logs. Bake for 5 minutes on each side. Let cool on a wire rack. Store in an airtight container. Well-wrapped cookies may be frozen.

Makes about 6½ dozen cookies

GIFT PACKAGES FOR COOKIES

Remember to separate cookie types, except in an open dish or basket, so the flavors won't mingle.

❧ Fill cellophane bags two thirds full with cookies and tie with natural raffia or ribbons. This is the appealing and speedy presentation I use the most.

❧ Line small white cardboard gift or bakery boxes with waxed tissue or paper (so grease marks won't show), fill with cookies, top with a small, beautiful paper doily, and tie with a pastel-and-white striped ribbon.

❧ Present elegant cookies in a pretty, one-of-a-kind dish found for pennies in a garage sale.

❧ Present homey cookies in something offbeat, such as a clean rustic bucket lined with a dish towel.

❧ For a large group of people, line a handsome basket with a beautifully edged fine linen napkin and fill with cookies neatly arranged in groups. If the basket is quite deep, crush paper to put underneath the napkin. Tie a fat ribbon on the handle.

❧ Cover a cylindrical oatmeal cardboard container and its lid with gift-wrapping paper cut to fit and glued around it. Fill with cookies.

❧ For the holidays paint a basket with gold, silver, or copper paint, and line it with a festive plaid napkin that has a few metallic threads woven in. Fill with rolled cookies cut in holiday shapes.

❧ Paint a summertime basket in a refreshingly pale color that coordinates with a large floral print napkin. Line it with the napkin and fill with light, crisp cookies.

❧ Fill a Mason jar with cookies. Tie a grosgrain ribbon around the top, knot, and cut the ends short at an angle, rather than making a bow. Hang a handmade gift tag, artfully cut from a used greeting card.

❧ New or antique cookie jars and decorative old tins, a gift in themselves, will be doubly appreciated if filled with homemade cookies.

❧ To gift wrap a large single cookie, place it on a sturdy rectangle of mat board, foam-core board, or paper-covered cardboard cut 1 inch larger than the cookie. Tightly wrap it with a large sheet of cellophane, tape it closed in the back, and tie with coordinating ribbons.

❧ Wrap cookies in waxed paper or plastic wrap and place in a brown paper lunch bag. Tie with natural-colored raffia or a red gingham bow.

❧ Logs of chilled icebox cookie dough may be gift wrapped in brown paper and tied with raffia or gift wrapped in beautiful paper and tied with ribbons, but should be chilled on receipt.

❧ Recycled glass jars with lids can be filled with drop cookie dough and festooned with an old-fashioned red-bordered label from the stationery store. Store them refrigerated.

TO MAIL COOKIES

Many cookies can be shipped in a sturdy box, as long as they are packed so that they don't rattle around. Avoid mailing thin, fragile cookies and any that should be refrigerated. Biscotti, shortbread, brownies, and molasses, ginger, and sugar cookies are particularly good for shipping. Biscotti, especially, are famous for their long shelf life. The dryer the cookie the longer it will keep.

The most foolproof way to pack cookies for shipping is to place pairs of cookies with their flat, bottom sides together and wrap each pair with plastic wrap. Line the bottom of a sturdy box with bubble pack and a layer of cookies, and repeat the process. I also have successfully shipped cookies gift wrapped in cellophane bags, then wrapped in bubble pack and placed in a box filled with (recycled) Styrofoam chips. Air-popped popcorn (hold the butter and salt), crumbled brown paper, or newspaper can also be used as a packing filler.

TEMPLATE AND PATTERN GUIDE

Rolled cookies can be cut out with cutters or template guides. To make templates trace or draw the design onto sheer paper or photocopy it. Place a large sheet of carbon paper, shiny side down, on a piece of posterboard slightly larger than the design. Tape the carbon paper at the corners to hold it in place. Center the traced design on top of the carbon paper; tape it at the corners. Use a ball-point pen or soft lead pencil to firmly retrace the design so that the lines transfer to the posterboard. Remove the design and carbon paper. Cut out the template with sturdy scissors. Use a push pin to mark key details such as eyes. This will provide guidance when decorating baked cookies.

Lightly flour the template before using to prevent it from sticking to the dough. Center the template on top of the rolled-out dough (which should be on a cutting board or baking sheet so that knife nicks won't damage a counter or tabletop). Use an X-acto knife or a small, sharp-pointed knife to cleanly cut the dough at the template edge. Mark holes in the dough with a toothpick to indicate key details. Remove the template and the excess dough.

MAIL-ORDER GUIDE

American Spoon Foods
P.O. Box 566
Petoskey, MI 49770
1-800-222-5886
Black walnuts, wild pecans,
hickory nuts, butternuts, dried
berries, jams, jellies, and preserves. Catalogue available.

The Chocolate Gallery
34 West 22nd Street
New York, NY 10010
1-212-675-CAKE
Natural flavorings, peppermint
oil, royal icing flowers, dragées,
sprinkles. Catalogue available.

Dean & Deluca
560 Broadway
New York, NY 10012
1-800-221-7714, ext. 270
Vanilla extracts, fine chocolate,
gourmet ingredients. Catalogue $3.

**King Arthur Flour Baker's
    Catalogue**
P.O. Box 876
Norwich, VT 05055
1-800-827-6836
Baking supplies and equipment,
flours, maple sugar, boiled cider.
Catalogue available.

La Cuisine
323 Cameron Street
Alexandria, VA 22314
1-800-521-1176
Baking supplies and equipment,
natural flavorings, gold and silver
leaf, gilder's tips, wooden molds.
Catalogue available.

Maid of Scandinavia
32–44 Raleigh Avenue
Minneapolis, MN 55416
1-800-328-6722
Baking supplies and equipment,
cookie presses, baking parchment,
doilies, colored tissue paper.
Catalogue available.

The Silo
44 Upland Road
New Milford, CT 06776
1-203-355-0300
Baking supplies and equipment,
decorative baking pans, jams
and jellies.

Williams-Sonoma
Mail Order Department
P.O. Box 7456
San Francisco, CA 94120-7456
1-800-541-2233
Baking equipment, fine vanilla
extract, gourmet ingredients,
madeleine pans. Catalogue available.

Wilton Enterprises
2240 West 57th Street
Woodridge, IL 60517
1-708-963-7100
Baking supplies, pastry bags and
tips, baking parchment, paste food
colors, meringue powder, cookie
cutters. Catalogue available.

Wood's Cider Mill
RFD 2, P.O. Box 477
Springfield, VT 05156
1-802-263-5547
Boiled cider, maple sugar.
Catalogue available.

Zabar's
2245 Broadway
New York, NY 10024
1-212-787-2000
Baking supplies and equipment,
electric pizzelle irons, small ice
cream scoops, knives. Catalogue
available.

INDEX

TABLE OF EQUIVALENTS

The exact equivalents in the following tables
have been rounded for convenience.

US/UK

oz=ounce
lb=pound
in=inch
ft=foot
tbl=tablespoon
fl oz=fluid ounce
qt=quart

Metric

g=gram
kg=kilogram
mm=millimeter
cm=centimeter
ml=milliliter
l=liter

Weights

US/UK	Metric
1 oz	30 g
2 oz	60 g
3 oz	90 g
4 oz (¼ lb)	125 g
5 oz (⅓ lb)	155 g
6 oz	185 g
7 oz	220 g
8 oz (½ lb)	250 g
10 oz	315 g
12 oz (¾ lb)	375 g
14 oz	440 g
16 oz (1 lb)	500 g
1 ½ lb	750 g
2 lb	1 kg
3 lb	1.5 kg

Oven Temperatures

Fahrenheit	Celsius	Gas
250	120	½
275	140	1
300	150	2
325	160	3
350	180	4
375	190	5
400	200	6
425	220	7
450	230	8
475	240	9
500	260	10